HEBRIDEAN GURKHA

WALKING THE OUTER ISLES

Neil Griffiths

CUALANN PRESS

ISBN 10: 0-9544416-6-4
ISBN 13: 978-0-9544416-6-1

First Edition 2005

British Library Cataloguing in Publication Data. A catalogue record of this book is available at the British Library.

Printed by Bell & Bain, Glasgow

Published by Cualann Press Limited, 6 Corpach Drive, Dunfermline,
KY12 7XG Scotland
Tel/Fax 01383 733724
Email: cualann@btinternet.com
Website: www.cualann.com

BIOGRAPHICAL NOTE

Neil Griffiths is the author of *Gurkha Reiver*: *Walking the Southern Upland Way,* and *Gurkha Highlander: Walking Mallaig to Stonehaven.* Both books were highly acclaimed in reviews and by Joanna Lumley, much-loved actress and the daughter of a Gurkha Major. Now living in Edinburgh, Griffiths is a former soldier and Fleet Street journalist who has written for *The Guardian*, *The Scotsman*, *The Herald, The Sunday Post, The Sun, The Glasgow Evening Times, The Edinburgh Evening News*, many magazines and weekly papers. He is perhaps best known as the press officer for the Scottish Poppy Appeal, The Royal British Legion Scotland, The Gurkha Welfare Trust (Scotland) and as editor of the Legion's journal, *The Scottish Legion News*.

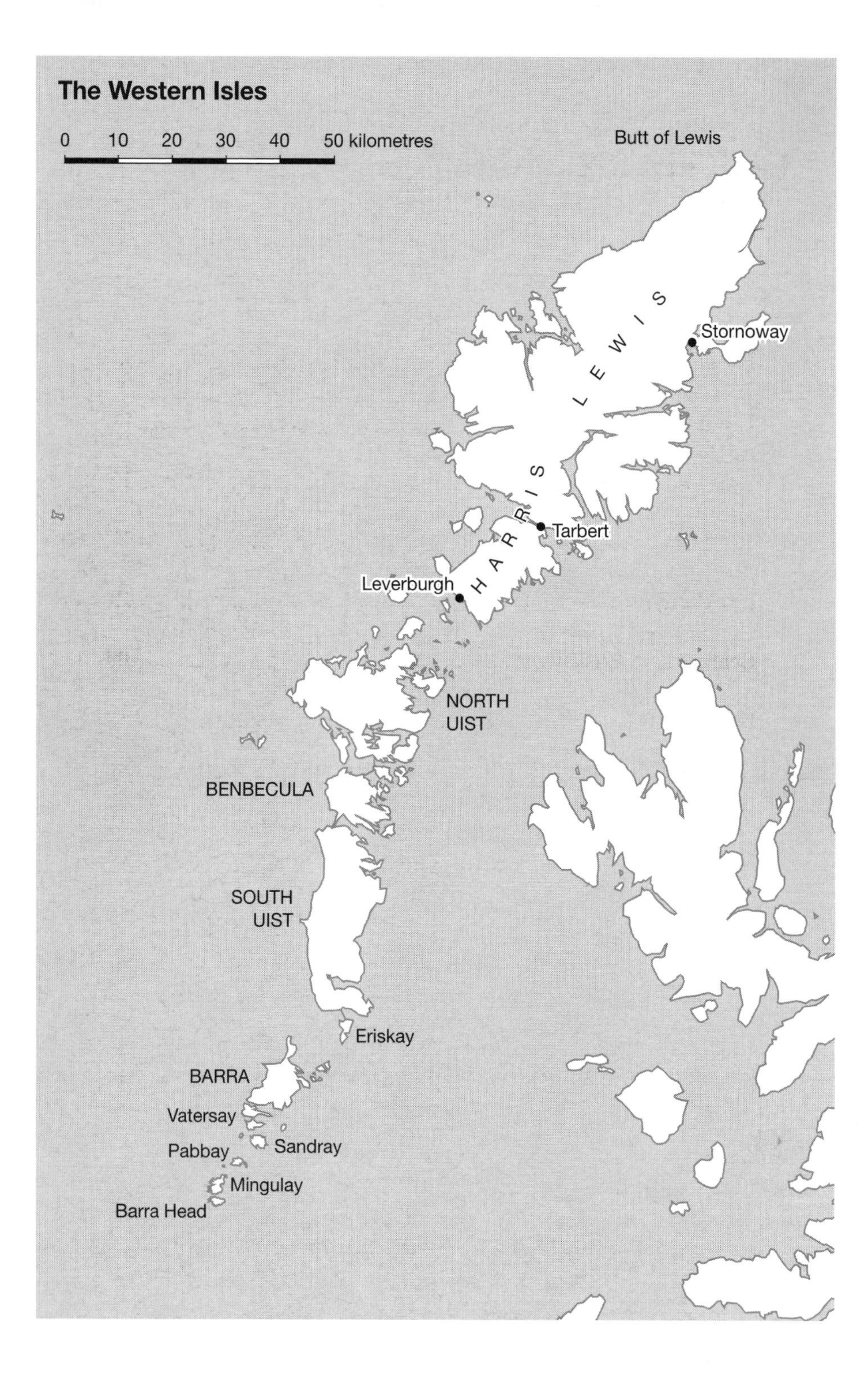
The Western Isles
0 10 20 30 40 50 kilometres
Butt of Lewis
LEWIS
Stornoway
HARRIS
Tarbert
Leverburgh
NORTH UIST
BENBECULA
SOUTH UIST
Eriskay
BARRA
Vatersay
Sandray
Pabbay
Mingulay
Barra Head

CONTENTS

INTRODUCTION

The necklace of isles that lies off Scotland's North West is always on the edge of our map, history and consciousness. A land without trees but soaked in its own culture, it is both apart but part of us.

When my Gurkha team marched through, it seemed initially that there could be few similarities. To our surprise we discovered so many links between these flatlands and the high Himalaya that the whole endeavour seemed pre-planned by anthropologists. Everything in Nepal, from standing stones, military past and belief in Fate, to survival in the face of cruel landlords and a tradition of storytelling, was reproduced in the Hebrides. Even the necessity to travel to seek a decent life was a shared history. That social events included drink, dance and song was welcome, but that they included the pipes and whisky was fantastic!

We were to experience the Outer Isles in a series of dramatic cameos, with each successive act out-doing the other. God, as the ultimate director, gave us a treat. The folk of Lewis, Harris, the Uists and finally Barra showed us kindness, as well as kindred spirit, so great that we fell in love with all of them. If that seems an exaggeration, do this walk yourself with five Gurkhas. I promise you, nothing, apart from perhaps the weather, will be different.

Despite the fact that 99% of the country has never met a Gurkha, the British still know enough to recognise and salute the smiling men from Nepal who have served the Crown for nearly 200 years. If this book half explains why we admire them, it will have done its job. It is merely a tale of five of them in the Outer Hebrides for a week but I hope it demonstrates why the legendary Gurkha has such a special place in the nation's affections.

Joanna Lumley has long supported our annual treks in Scotland and while every Gurkha can say 'Absolutely Fabulous', they also know she's a daughter of the Regiment, 6th Gurkha Rifles. The memory of her father, Major James Lumley, Gurkha officer and Chindit, has not been forgotten by the Brigade of Gurkhas. Ms Lumley recently came across her father's

Gurkhali phrasebook (written by the famous Brigadier R. G. Leonard) which included the necessary: 'And I, in turn, drew my kukri and killed him,' along with, 'I found forty men gambling behind a locked door.' This, I feel, tells us a lot about our Nepalese friends. Thanks, Joanna, for your wonderful support.

'Beannaich na Gurkhas!', 'Bless the Gurkhas!', uttered so often in the Hebrides, still rings in my ears. Or 'Jai Gurkhali!', the Gurkhas own blessing.

Neil Griffiths
Edinburgh

Overleaf. Barra Head: Feat of endurance, with flagged-up spirits

CHAPTER ONE

THE BUTT OF LEWIS TO STORNOWAY

'Neil, the weather get better? Does it always blow here? This is good?' asked Suk earnestly, his eyes shining. Colleagues, Nugendra, Ram, Kesh and Dhal grinned at each other under their baseball caps, pleased to be ready to move. They even shared the same big smile, though Kesh was disappointed to learn that despite the many bobbing sea birds, there were no penguins today. Ram was still capable of muddling the Northern Isles with Northern Ireland while Suk would to be shocked to learn that seawater, absolutely all of it, was salty.

The clouds hung heavy over the shifting Atlantic, like a grey watercolour sponged with black. A thin wind blew in our faces no matter which way we turned. The group was standing at the Butt of Lewis, the most northerly point of the Outer Hebrides, the edge of Europe, where the land meets the sea and the sea runs into the sky. My little team of Gurkhas eyed the view with interest, scanning the hinterland as if on a military exercise. Unaccustomed to the sea, never mind an ocean on three sides, they had rarely encountered such low horizons, but seemed unfazed. Since they'd taken the Queen's rupee they'd seen Belize, Kenya and Brunei. This was just another patrol in foreign parts. Today they were their usual bright, composed selves, ready to laugh and march 160 miles south.

Dramatically spearing the skyline was a lighthouse whose long neck rose gracefully above us. My brother Ewen came trudging over from the cliff edge, where he'd been photographing gannets, his big boots clumping. 'Right, let's be having you!' he called in mock drill sergeant's voice.

'Tayah, ketaharu? Ready lads?' I asked. 'Let's go!'

The initial mud track quickly developed into a metalled road. The trek would not be demanding on the lungs but would punish the feet. The route was nearly all on tarmac and I knew from old how numbing this could be, but if we were to complete the hike in seven days we had no option. The road down the isles began here and, albeit with a couple of ferries, stretched to the most southerly point of the Outer Hebrides, Barra Head. 'Hillboys to Barra Boys' was a later headline that perfectly described our party, the Hebridean Gurkhas.

The clouded light was soft, somehow mineral, as if in a land without trees: it would always be gentle. Even on a near-filthy day there was a touch of the untouchable, unquantifiable Hebridean magic in the air. The few fields were long but narrow, and mostly knee deep in wild flowers. The first cottage had several hundred peats heaped against an outer wall like neatly piled tiles of chocolate. Though this was July, smoke was peeling from a chimney before being snatched away in the breeze.

The first township, Eoropaidh (pronounced Yorrerpee), surprised us. 'Look! A football stadium!' pointed Dhal laughing. Sure enough, a cute wee football stand stood beside a smoothly cut and rollered pitch. It was as unexpected as a NASA launch pad.

'Why would they have one here?' asked Dhal, reading a sign that implied that this was the home to the legendary Ness FC.

'Got me there,' replied Ewen. 'You'd think that it would make sense to have placed it more centrally instead of right up here.'

'What's this doing here?' I called to a figure down the road clad in blue coveralls. The guy stopped mid stride as if caught mid crime before strolling over, tugging at his sheaf of fair hair. 'That's the ground of Ness Football Club,' he declared. 'Fabulous team. Won the Highland Amateur four times. Used to play for it myself until my disciplinary problems.'

'Er, right. What happened?'

'We won the cup! Four times!'

'No, I meant your disciplinary problems.'

He was now only inches away, giving out heavy vibes that this wasn't a very clever question. On his hams were tattoos that proclaimed violence, death and – perversely – honour. The latter was misspelled. 'Er, this is the group of Gurkhas that is walking to Barra Head,' I said, changing the subject.

'The stadium is owned by the whole community, not the community council, mind, the whole community,' he warned.

This is all my fault for opening my stupid mouth in the first place, I thought, wondering how long this would last. 'Right! We must be going,' I announced cheerfully.

'The local school uses it too,' our man called urgently as he realised we were off. 'Bye!'

The few homes were mostly modern bungalows, interspersed with sagging Victorian ruins like some bizarre exhibitions of architectural decay. Although about ten o'clock on a Saturday morning, nobody stirred. This surprised us as the Western Isles' lifestyle was in my mind's eye: early to bed, early to rise, lots of fresh air and fixing the croft, not slumbering until lunch like a teenager on the dole. But I was wrong. Being from rural backgrounds, Gurkhas themselves are naturally early risers, used to making the most of daylight, but, it has to be said, are as keen on loafing as the rest of us.

Eoropaidh has two roads, more a loop really (which was why we'd missed the grandstand on our drive to the start) but once we were through the township, there was only one long road running to the skyline like an exercise in perspective. Things livened up when we hit the A857. This is the slim road that runs down the northern flank of Lewis, before turning south midway and heading down to the only town in the Hebrides, Stornoway. 'Is this what you call a 'string' road?' I had asked a local.

'This is what we call the main road,' he had chuckled back.

To our right the land sloped down to the sea in narrow green fields but to our left, and stretching to the grey horizon was a dark brooding peat moor, pocked with hundreds of lochans filled with motionless black water. The map showed many more, but the wallowing sky dominated the landscape like a Dutch painting, swirling and soaring, immeasurably big.

The road rose and fell like a black ribbon stretched across a huge untidy parcel of heather.

They may be nerveless soldiers but Gurkhas are heroically self-confident models and completely fearless before a camera. Hopelessly sentimental too, they can get nostalgic about yesterday, so it was no surprise that we stopped after barely twenty minutes to take group pictures. That there had been several rolls of film given over to us posing before the lighthouse was irrelevant; there can never be too many pictures of the team.

Nugendra lined us up in front of an extraordinary stone bus shelter that looked like a prop from The Flintstones, except that it was several tons of genuine gneiss set in a star shape. This permitted travellers to huddle out of the wind by simply hiding behind the shelter. It, of course, might mean one couldn't see an oncoming bus, while the wind ensured you couldn't hear it either. A too-small roof, another slab of rock, indicated you wouldn't even keep dry. But it would never be blown away. Truly a masterpiece of product design. There were many of them too, indicating a loony sense of practicalities together with the real possibility of ferocious winter storms.

'Strange,' murmured Nugendra pensively. Perhaps Stonehenge was nothing more than a Mesolithic bus depot.

'I think that's enough now,' I pleaded but Ram was being induced by Suk into taking snaps of Suk with Suk's camera. This looked like a serious error from where I was standing as it was obvious that Ram had no idea what he was doing. Strangely, it is the Gurkha photographers who always appear embarrassed, not their subject. The model, with his puffed-out chest and Kodak smile, is on familiar ground. But cameras require a level of expertise that only comes with practice, and ineptitude can hit a man right in the ego. Gurkhas love gadgets and you can bet that the camera was using a technology you've barely heard about.

At 5'10" Nugendra was easily the tallest Gurkha I had ever come across, and well built too. Suk was nearly his height and strapping with it, while Kesh was lean and small. All were Gurungs, the clan some consider the original Gurkhas. All were riflemen who were serving with the 1st Battalion The Highlanders and based in Edinburgh. The whole of their hundred-strong unit, A Company, were Nepalese bar two British officers. Their green beret bore a patch of red tartan behind the famous crossed kukri cap badge. Ramkumar was of the Magar clan and unit piper. An old-school Gurkha, he had served for nearly twenty years and had the unyielding muscular build of the true hillboy. His near-shaven head exuded an air of toughness which made one quite forget he was barely 5’3”. His English was limited, but though he could hardly deliver a whole sentence in our language, Ram had no difficulty in communicating, and as a piper, would always be quick to make friends out here.

Our nonchalant heart and senior NCO was Sergeant Dhal Sahi of the Queen’s Gurkha Signals, an old friend and expert piper, who had accompanied me on two previous trans-Scotland marches. Dhal also shared the merry sense of humour of all the Nepalese hill people which either helped him out of trouble or got him into some of the most extraordinary scrapes imaginable.

At forty-five, I wasn’t quite twice the age of our youngest, Kesh, who was just twenty-three, but knew from experience that if I gave my colleagues free rein, their instinctive 140 per minute pace would kick in and shake the flesh from my bones. It would always be like riding with young horses who were ever ready to break into a smoking gallop. The other *gora*, European, who made up the walking team was my thirty-four-year-old brother, Ewen, to whom a fast pace was of no concern. A Gurkha corporal once pointed admiringly at Ewen’s disappearing form with the words: ‘He very fit man.’ Another came to a more stern conclusion and wanted to know why he wasn’t in the Army. We were a team though, and went at the pace of the slowest – guess whose?

The road took us through a number of tiny townships, no more than a string of bungalows surrounded by rusting washing machines and fridges. These continued for a couple of identical miles where taped-up telegraph wires tangled above us in freestyle exuberance. Then, as we passed the last dumped motor, the moorland opened up again, and the process repeated itself. Though the land remained achingly bleak the peat cuttings

Overleaf. *Left:* Sukbahadur Gurung. Our comedy department.
***Right:* Nugendra Gurung, the world’s biggest Gurkha.**

HEBRIDEAN GURKHA

became steadily more numerous. Even the traffic picked up. There was an old-time drill hall, signposted as 'A Company. The Highlanders', a TA unit, but it gave the guys a bit of a shock to be passing what seemed to be their Company HQ.

'When I was a young soldier on exercise in Wales, we came across an old car whose number plate had the initials of a friend,' I grinned. 'Of course, I ripped it off, put in my pack and gave it to him later!' Suk gave me what I liked to think was a look of awe. 'I'm not altogether sure it was an abandoned car, come to think of it,' I added conspiratorially. Suk's expression changed as comprehension sank in. 'You! Thief!' he laughed, never taking his eyes off me. To this day I'm not entirely sure that this story went down quite the way I'd hoped.

'Hello!' beckoned an elderly woman from her porch. 'You'll be the Gurkhas?' We trooped over to be given a fiver. 'I read all about ye in the *Stornoway Gazette*, an' I've been looking out for ye,' she declared, smiling through thick specs.

'Can I introduce you? This is Suk, Nugendra, Kesh, Ram and Dhal,' I said. Though friendly, Gurkhas are notoriously shy and would have remained beaming and nodding before it occurred to them to speak. There was an answering smile and then a quizzical look from the lady. Something was wrong. Then it dawned; she wondered who the heck I was! The big bloke with the funny accent was as alien to her as the guys from Nepal. Perhaps she thought I was a Gurkha too? Here we had found a different air, light, landscape, religion, history, folklore and even language: all the characteristics of being abroad. Of course, I was foreign too.

From here to Barvas, the township at our sixteen mile mark where the road suddenly headed south, we were to be stopped regularly and cheerfully by the old and young with donations for the Gurkha Welfare Trust. Those in cars received a windscreen sticker and the others a simple lapel sticker but each was an occasion of mutual goodwill. The generosity was extraordinary.

'They are good people,' said Nugendra knowingly. The team began to realise that it had come to a special part of the world.

'Look! Man in hedge!' pointed Suk. Sure enough, there was a figure ahead, lying on his belly, attempting to photograph us through his garden hedge. He stood up sheepishly as the boys goggled.

'Thought I'd try and catch you out,' he mumbled.

'Oh, an ambush?' I asked.

'Aye, that sort of thing,' he nodded.

Ewen and I rolled our eyes but the guys seemed nonplussed.

By the time we stopped for lunchtime sandwiches we had been offered tea and biscuits several times over. My famous self restraint had permitted us to take advantage of only three such offers. The kitchens were all immaculate and could have featured in any home improvement magazine. Those overlooking the sea would witness some of the world's most spectacular sunsets throughout the summer – and quite possibly some of the planet's grimmest winter nights too.

'Ciya?' I asked Suk, as we sat cross-legged on a deserted garage forecourt. 'Tea' in Nepali is ciya (pronounced chee-ah) and Gurkhas tend to swamp it in milk and sugar as if to take on board as much energy as possible. Suk was no exception and held a cup to my poured flask before flooding it with milk to the point where I wondered why I'd bothered to keep it hot at all. It is in India, south of Nepal, that pronunciation shifts and the beverage becomes that good old Hindi word, *char*. North of the Himalaya, it becomes that good old Chinese word, *cha*.

I'd made a small fool of myself over Suk's name when I had asked his company 2ic, Captain Guptaman Gurung, what it meant. Somehow he had assumed I had asked how Suk was. 'Happy!' Guptaman replied.

'Good grief, I'll be getting the Sleepy, Dopey and Grumpy next,' I thought, an idea that received a sharp set back when Suk and Nugendra – the world's biggest Gurungs – turned up the next day. In fact, Suk is short for *sukrabar*, Friday, after the day of his birth.

'Friday's child works hard for his living,' I had explained: 'I was born on a Friday too.'

'Ma bihibar,' I'm Thursday's, added Nugendra.

'Thursday's child has far to go,' put in Ewen. 'It's from what we call a nursery rhyme, for children.' There was one of those blank looks that mean, forget it, in any language.

'In old day, what did people eat here?' asked Dhal, who like all his colleagues, were from an agricultural background that bordered on subsistence level, and knew how to read a landscape.

'It was never easy, a lot starved,' I said. Ness, in fact, had a peculiar and surviving source of protein, the young gannet, whose flesh hereabouts is called 'guga' and gives rise to the annual Guga Hunt when the men of Ness sail forty miles north to an islet called Sula Sgeir to hunt the seabird. Sula Sgeir is, not surprisingly, desolately remote. Every autumn a team still returns with around 2,000 young birds. The demand is huge. 'Oh!' winced a local when I later asked him if he'd ever tasted guga, 'Salty, very salty!' The pronunciation was almost Gurkha Hunt which brought wry smiles. Despite protests, the hunt received special exemption from the 1954 Wild Birds Protection Act permitting it to continue. To this day the Scottish Executive hands out an annual dispensation.

I told this tale expecting interest, giggles or approval but the boys merely accepted it as part of the natural order. The resource was there, people were fed and there were still plenty of gannets, weren't there? It told me something about the folk of the Isles though.

Twelve miles to Sula Sgeir's east is North Rona which was considered such a hell hole that it was once offered as a penal settlement to the Government by one Sir James Matheson, the then owner of all Lewis. The offer, one of the very few of Sir James's recorded acts of generosity, was refused.

The urgency to keep moving pressed us on, a necessity made monotonous by the unremitting peat moors. The traffic included a number of ordinary cars with home-made trailers for peat. The area was clearly very rich in the stuff with a large number of cuttings visible from the road. The peats lay on the heather like sods of Bourneville, not in piles but spread out like playing cards to dry. When the peat is dug up, boulder clay is exposed, the clay having been glacially deposited on the gneiss bedrock during the last Ice Age. The result is called 'skinned ground' or 'gearradh' which forms the basis of a soil which, when mixed with shell-sand and seaweed, becomes quite fertile and provides the basis for crofting.

'What are these?' asked the ever curious Suk.

'Peats, they burn them up here like coal. They don't give as much heat though.'

We stopped at the roadside to finger a couple and were surprised that they had dried almost as hard as wood. You can tap them.

'They give much smoke?' asked Suk uncertainly.

'Yeah, there's a poem about how the peats first warm themselves before they warm you,' I answered.

'More children's songs?' he grinned.

'Yeah, a poem really, but don't read anything into it!'

'Makes your face black,' Suk said knowingly, holding a peat. 'You burn these in house and the smoke makes you black.' For a second, I wondered what he meant and then I remembered photos of the soot-blackened faces of Nepalese hillmen, and had a flash of insight into the old Hebridean black house, *tigh dubh*, which was windowless and must have blackened anyone who lived within. There weren't even chimneys, just a hole in the thatch – and not over the fire itself, which would have allowed rain to fall on to the hearth. I wondered to myself how Suk had surmised this just from holding a single peat for a brief moment.

'Strange,' concluded Nugendra. 'In my home village we have no fuel except little wood. Everything has to be carried and we have no coal either.' It was as if one always had a choice of peat or coal, and someone had blundered by not organising at least coal for Nepal. The gods obviously needed reproaching for having been so benevolent to these far-flung isles who only had to dig up a field to be warm, while overlooking the deprivations of Himalayan communities.

'Only the women in the Outer Isles carried anything on their back. It was practically the law. Men were not allowed to do any housework either. Men helped cut them but the peats were carried home only by women. All the old photos show only women with creels on their backs,' I explained. 'When soldiers came back from the First World War some of them began to carry peats. Everyone reckoned they'd been traumatised by the trenches!'

'Our women do all the housework,' put in Dhal smugly. 'But everyone carries the loads, even the kids. As a little boy, we all carried stuff up the hill.' He mimed lifting a load on to his back by imaginary tump-lines across his forehead. Hillboys prefer to carry their luggage like this and develop an extraordinary musculature as a consequence. Nepal has precious few beasts of burden and to imagine circumstances where every single content of my childhood home had arrived there solely by family muscle is utterly beyond me.

The map showed a series of townships. Many of the countless lochans had names, while spattered all over the entire map was the word 'shieling' referring to summer huts used mostly by shepherds. The names on the map were nearly always in Gaelic only but the road signs announcing townships' names were in the anglicised form. This was not a problem; for instance, Nis was Ness and Barabhas was Barvas, the translations giving us a clue as to their pronunciation. But it was doubly ironic; of the 126 place names in Lewis, 99 are Norse and only nine are Gaelic.

One might presume that the original Ordnance Survey men in the 1840s might have been indifferent or slipshod in transcribing Gaelic names, resulting in misinterpretations such as 'Gleneagles' which has nothing to do with eagles but refers to *eaglais* or church. In fact, it's amazing that so many of the Gaelic names survived at all when the surveyors were English speakers, and the majority of the people they checked with spoke Gaelic and had little or no written education. Queen Victoria's diaries are full of well-intentioned but misspelled place names.

Having threatened all morning, the rain began to patter down in a thin, irritating drizzle that I knew was called 'sma' rain' in west-coast Scotland. You've got to laugh when a nation has developed quite so many terms for rain. Gurkhas call it *pani*, the term for water and tears. Not having a word for the sea, they call it *kala pani*, the black water. Pani is a Sanskrit word still used by Romanies for water and by all the modern Hindi languages. To my surprise, I once came across it being used by farm folk in Cumberland where it had been a dialect word for unknown generations. We had been warned that the Western Isles has a weather system all of its own, with the prevailing winds blowing in filthy weather from the Atlantic, as if on rails, from the south west to the north east, which can often miss the mainland. Consequently, the London or Glasgow-based met-men can promise an excellent day when giving a general UK or Scottish weather picture, but overlook the clouds on the Isles' horizon. This can be seriously misleading. There is both an Iranian and Iraqi blessing, 'May your skies always have clouds in them' which implies that they, poor folk, do not enjoy the usual Hebridean weather fronts.

'Do you have goddess of travellers?' asked Suk, grinning at the blotched sky.

'We have St Christopher, but we're not sure he ever existed.'

'We have Drolma. Perhaps we should pray?' he chuckled as if the goddess was his favourite comedian. There are some 300 million Hindu deities. Was Drolma the right one? Long journeys on foot are an inescapable part of Nepalese life and many travellers prayed to Dromla. Perhaps she's too busy? Religion plays an important role in Nepalese life and no understanding of Nepal would be complete without at least a passing familiarity with some of it. Gurkhas tend to be pragmatic about the finer points of religious observance but perhaps that explains why Buddhism and Hinduism thrive alongside each other in Nepal. It certainly explains why nineteenth century Gurkhas were so effective in India; they did not need to stop every few hours on the march to perform any rites, and in a subcontinent over-endowed with such interruptions, this was a whopping military advantage.

For country folk everywhere, superstition runs in close parallel with organised religion. Here in the Western Isles is a residual belief in fairies very similar to that found in the high Himalaya, where the inexplicable is made explicable through the supernatural. Your child falls ill, a calf dies, the crops fail, all for no reason until seen in the context of an unpredictable spirit world. Hence a young hillboy will have his ears pierced, not for vanity's sake but because the piercings make him physically imperfect and less likely to be abducted by the fairies.

'Our fairies are both good and bad. There is a story about a girl with a withered leg who was working on the peats just here,' I pointed, 'when she heard a fairy's voice coming from just over the rise: "Monday, Tuesday, Wednesday … what comes next?" After a moment's pause, the girl called "Thursday." She wasn't sure that she'd done the right thing and anxiously hurried home. By the time she got there, everyone was astonished to see her withered leg had healed. The fairies had done her a good deed. The next day her sister decided to go to the same peat cutting and see if the fairies would grant her a wish. Sure enough, she heard a fairy voice floating over the heather: "One, two, three, four ... " She couldn't resist interrupting and shouted: " Five!" Suddenly her leg became withered. The fairies had felt insulted. And that is how the fairies are. You can't tell what they're going to do. Sometimes good and sometimes bad, but they should always to be treated with caution.'

This tale had our boys' eyes switching back and forth between me and the moor as if seeking confirmation, with that look of half-delight you see on the face of someone discovering a hidden secret. There were nods and murmurs of agreement at the conclusion. That Scots shared the very same oral traditions of story-telling as they did, of keeping alive the tales of the old, really hit home. I half suspected Suk was going to blurt that wee boy request: 'Again!'

'You know, at Dunvegan Castle in Skye, the MacLeod's ancient stronghold not far from here, there is what's called The Fairy Flag,' I continued, getting into my stride. 'In the 1930s the clan chief, Sir Reginald MacLeod, had it examined by an expert from the Victoria and Albert Museum in London who announced it was probably brought to Britain by a Viking. The clan chief drew himself up to his full height and declared: "You may believe that but I know it was given to an ancestor by the fairies." The expert replied: "Sir, I bow to your superior knowledge."'

The boys howled with glee as if this was the funniest, wittiest, most thrilling story they'd ever heard – and, no, they weren't being sarcastic. Why had I never before, I wondered, mentioned to Gurkhas Gaeldom's love of folk tales involving fairies, second sight, kelpies and snow giants, until our boots were actually crossing the earth of the Outer Hebrides? Was there something within being unlocked by simply being here? Dr Johnson and Boswell on their 1773 visit to Skye were constantly struck by the prevalence of superstition, bowls of milk offerings to a grey-bearded man, and above all a tendency to embroider the truth, not actually lying but more as though exactness was something foreign to them.

Perhaps it was a belief system which enabled blame to be laid and a matter closed. One thing I do know, there is at least one wartime official RAF Crash Report which describes, very pragmatically, the Uist wreck of an Andover aircraft as having some of its cables and most of its dials 'removed by the fairies' as it lay unattended on the machair. The report never got as far as the Air Ministry but was sat on by someone in metropolitan la-dee-da Inverness who presumably knew his Whitehall masters might not accept such a conclusion as entirely scientific. And what if it had got out that the little people were sabotaging the war effort?

Gurkhas believe it is unlucky to marry in July or August, to leave home on a Saturday or arrive on a Tuesday. Clothes bought on a Monday should be destroyed, or at least a bit of their fluff burned, while the number eight is their number thirteen. To dream of a man in white clothes means a death in the family while dreams of sickness, perversely, portend happiness and health. These are only some brief examples of the countless superstitions which a Gurkha must observe if he is to keep the world intact, and happily co-exist with the spiritual beliefs of his religion. In this they are, yet again, like us. Remember, we're the people that believe in horoscopes, avoid going under ladders, trust rabbit paws and throw salt over our shoulders. Mind you, I don't believe all that rubbish. We're real cynics, we Leos.

The boredom of road-walking in an unchanging landscape was reduced by letting our minds roam elsewhere. The A857's only diversion was conversation and we were short of neither breath nor topics.

No-one can travel this road, this stretched-out spine of Lewis, without passing several lonely war memorials standing silent sentinel to the terrible losses of the Great War. Out of a population of nearly 30,000, more than 6,000 men and women from Lewis and Harris served and almost 1,100 lost their lives. From the township of Port Mholair fifty-five served, ten lost their lives and seven were badly wounded; of the fifty-one from Port Nan Guiran eleven were killed and four wounded; from Ard fourteen out of sixteen servicemen died. All normal figures. The memorials, of course, list only the dead.

We stopped to inspect them all, often entering a tidy enclosure through a neat gate to read the names on the plaque. While most were Seaforth Highlanders there was a preponderance of sailors which, we guessed, reflected the islanders' natural inclination to serve at sea. Some were from Canadian units which recalled pre-War emigration but bore

Overleaf. *Left:* Sergeant Dhalbahadur Sahi, our senior NCO.
***Right:* Ewen, pacesetter and Common Sense Department.**

witness that they had not been forgotten in the land of their birth.

There was one frequent date of death, 1st January 1919, which seemed to be an error until you knew the story. An armed yacht named the *Iolaire*, bringing returned servicemen home to Lewis for Hogmanay, had sunk outside Stornoway and 205 were drowned in the tragedy. They fell on the very last lap of their war. All the men knew each other and many were related. Some had been fishermen before the war and had made the approach hundreds of times. The captain, however, had never navigated a ship into Stornoway harbour at night. The passengers began to voice concern that the *Iolaire* was on a course that would drive her on to a notorious reef known as Biastan Thoilm – the Beasts of Holm. When the disaster struck, high seas prevented the approach of rescue ships. The Isles were numb with grief.

The terrible years of wartime, with the constant fear that a loved one would be killed or maimed, had ended when telegrams were stuck on Post Office windows which read: 'His Majesty's Government is pleased to inform the nation that Kaiser Wilhelm II, having abdicated, an Armistice has been signed, bringing hostilities between Great Britain and Germany to an end as from 11 a.m. GMT on 11 November 1918. God Save The King.' A sense of relief flooded the Isles as a future was suddenly visible. Old men began to repair boats and herring nets in readiness for the return of their sons. Young women whose sweet hearts had survived began to make plans for their weddings.

Then came the shattering news. Bunting was quickly taken down, hilltop bonfires remained unlit and whole families asked themselves how they could go on living. For a brief moment there had been the prospect of home, peace and family, but it was cruelly snatched away. Men who imagined they might meet their end in Flanders were to fall on the very shores of Lewis. The irony only made it harder to bear and for some survivors and family the shock was so great they never got over it.

Nearly 200,000 Gurkhas served the Crown in World War I, both on the Western Front and in Iraq. Today under lowering Atlantic skies our boys took time to honour their Hebridean colleagues with a mute intensity that was beyond religion. Gurkhas are never unmoved by commemoration of the war dead, whom they regard as heroes, and their reverence was practically poetic despite the absence of ceremony.

Campbell McRoberts, our support driver, was waiting for us in the rain at Barvas in what seemed to be the front of yet another deserted garage, surrounded by bubbling puddles. As a Rangers man it had broken Campbell's heart to have to drive a Volkswagen Caravelle minibus that was bright green, though we were delighted that Arnold Clark had given us a substantial discount for its hire, green or no. It was around 2 p.m. when we trooped up the rain-splashed road and leapt into the vehicle's dry seats, out of the wet and wind.

'How're the feet, Neil?' he asked.

'Hmm, I'm certainly feeling the pace,' I studied my boots accusingly. This was going to be a long haul. Lewis was harder work than I had imagined and I felt not just an unexpected wave of fatigue but a slight sense of depression. This was only the first day. Are my, ahem, thirteen stones too heavy for my forty-five-year old knees on this surface and at this pace?

'What about you, Dhal?'

Dhal grunted before announcing he was going to stay in the van. Eight months earlier he had snapped his Achilles tendon and was under strict instructions not to over-do it on Hebridean Gurkha. His long-term health must not be endangered but one of the benefits of walking on roads was that Dhal could be picked up by Campbell whenever necessary.

The boys gulped energy drinks and studied the map as the rain outside changed from a steady downpour to squalling sheets which the wind caught like rippling curtains.

'I got you *The Scotsman*. There's a big article about you lot complete with photos!' Campbell said, unfolding a copy from the dashboard. Four sets of hands tried to snatch it from him at the same time. 'Haud on, haud on! I got more than one copy!' he snapped like a schoolteacher before handing them out like class projects. With lunchtime newspaper deliveries being the norm hereabouts, I had asked Campbell to buy a handful in Stornoway as soon as they arrived. There under the headline 'The Hebrides? They're a piece of cake when you're from Nepal' was a double-page spread which announced the Gurkhas were on the march again and that everything would be a walk in the park.

'Aye, right! What could be easier than marching 160 miles on tarmac?' I muttered but no-one answered, their attention being totally absorbed by the photos of Ram and Suk in full ceremonial uniform.

'We did these last week,' explained Suk. 'We had photos of us with our feet in buckets too. They took all afternoon. Sometimes sitting, sometimes walking.' Ram poked his image as if it might react, a smile playing on his lips.

In the previous week I had met up with *The Scotsman*'s Susan Mansfield for a coffee and outlined our trek. I kind of blew this too. We had not previously met and I asked: 'Jane Mansfield?' Great start. I gave her an article I had written about the trek along with some photos of elderly former Gurkhas and today we had exactly the type of in-depth press coverage that we needed to raise our profile and bring in funds.

'I've been looking at these, trying to work out which of you was which,' commented Campbell.

'Surely you could see that the guy in the tartan, holding the pipes, might just be Ram?' asked Ewen sarcastically.

'Well, I didn't know it was Ram, I just thought it was a piper. And don't get cheeky with me unless you want to walk home tonight!' There was a roar of laughter as Campbell tried to bluff it out. 'And your picture doesn't even look like you, Suk, does it?'

'Yes,' Suk replied.

A silence fell over the team as they read the article together as the rain drummed to a crescendo on the roof. After a minute Nugendra idly slid open the side-door allowing a damp cold rush of air to blow in which caught the papers so that they flapped and strained like tethered gulls over the howls of the readers.

'Sorry,' he said quietly, albeit grinning, and closed the door. The shock intrusion of the elements was a rude reminder of what faced us on the road to Stornoway. What was worse was that we had to think about leaving right now.

'C'mon guys, let's go, aba an hos,' I said, stepping outside and into a generously proportioned puddle. Suk and Kesh jumped out too, pulling waterproof covers over their packs and tugging caps low. Trying to lift the guys, I slashed a big 'Z' in the air with my blackthorn stick and called:

'For I am Zorro, ze finest swordsman in all, er, Mexico!'

'What is Zorro!' asked Kesh, deadpan, as I realised I had the wrong audience.

'Zorro is the Spanish for fox and was the name given to a fictional character, who robbed from the rich … ' I started before it occurred to me that I wasn't really sure who Zorro was. 'Er, Ewen, what did Zorro actually do? Did he give to the poor or what?'

'You're the bloke going on about him!' Ewen pointed out, before affecting a Michael Palin-like voice. 'He taunted the capitalist repressors, the owners of the means of production, by merit of his dazzling swordsmanship. "Look at that! He was repressing me! Did you see that? Just then!"'

'Nice one, centurion!'

'Wrong film!' Ewen replied. 'That was *Holy Grail* not *Life of Brian.*'

'Oh, crucifixion is it? Teacher's pet!' The references brought uncomprehending grins to the lads as they clambered out of the minibus.

'Mero lauro kaha … ' Where is my stick ... I began, holding up the blackthorn, but a wave of laughter hit me like another squall. Now it was time for me to grin in miscomprehension. 'What?'

Ram in particular was doubling up in giggles. 'You say lauro but you mean loro!' he pointed at his groin and managed to gasp between paroxysms. 'Lauro is this!'

Ewen and I joined in the laughter. It was an incident that was referred to every time I picked up the blackthorn for the rest of the trip. When someone (normally Suk) would point meaningfully and declare it loro. Even when we met up for supper many months later, Suk couldn't help but remind us of the hilarious occasion when Neil Saheb muddled up his walking stick with his you know what.

We'd had our fill of these strange long villages with their show bungalows interspersed with derelicts and abandoned consumer goods ranging from cookers to cars. The people couldn't have been friendlier but were blind to the surrounding mess. We were not to know that this was

Overleaf. ***Left:*** **Kesh Gurung, the typical cheerful Gurkha.**
Right: **Ramkumar Bura, our bullet-headed piping friend.**

HEBRIDEAN GURKHA

practically universal throughout the Isles where space was aplenty but rubbish disposal costs prohibitive. But the Gurkhas loved them. Being from small villages themselves there was a natural affinity.

On the smeared horizon to our south lay the gentle hills of Harris set out in a row as if the humps of the Loch Ness monster, but our route was to take us slightly off due South, more South-South-East to Stornoway. If the road were a clock hand it would point at five. Starting in the Great Glen of Barvas, Gleann Mòr Bharabhais, was a ten-mile houseless tramp down a cross-island rift where both sides rose to block our view. There was absolutely nothing to see and the rain was unremitting; it was like walking down one long green ditch. 'I hope the guys aren't going to get too brassed off on their first day,' I said to Ewen.

'Nah, they'll be fine,' he replied warmly. Neither of us had any doubts; we were merely reassuring ourselves. As the leader, I was always aware that if this whole trek became a nightmare, I would be subject to that peculiar responsibility called blame. There was an overriding wish to just get this bit over which is not the sentiment that should pervade a walking holiday – and especially on Day One. Anyone with any experience of Scotland and long distance walking should be well aware that no-one should expect seven consecutive days of sunshine. A week of rain, of course, is possible.

'We'll keep going and see what's what,' I promised. The deluge never let up until the outskirts of Stornoway but progress, though monotonous, was easy. Even the spray of passing cars, the sheets of rain and the cold trickle down one's neck, failed to dampen our spirits. 'This is mad!' laughed Suk, his eyes half closed. Normally I walk to work along a path that follows the route of an old railway track made dangerous by high speed kamikaze cyclists that zip past missing me by inches – this was only slightly safer. Why is it, I wondered, that 'cycle path' sounds so similar to 'psychopath'?

While some suggest that to understand fully, a man requires you 'walk a mile in his shoes', I always found that walking alongside him a less clumsy alternative. This is a personal observation, my dears, but also true is that shared discomfort can be one of life's great bonders. A mutual look of rue holds more in it than any quick smile. Any train traveller knows this. When we found ourselves at last stepping past the gracious Victorian houses of Stornoway, looking like we'd swum there, it was with a calmness arrived at through an afternoon of such moments. It had seemed that the road itself was in spate. The Western Isles' rainfall must be measured in pints. Cars had frequently sounded their horns in greeting while one had stopped and presented each of us with a can of McEwans. The driver had read about us in the press and even had a copy for Dhal – which Ram was quick to claim in his absence.

Down at the harbour the team pushed open the door of the British Legion and found the place mobbed. A huge cheer went up as the drinkers turned to clap – responses that surprised and delighted us. 'What'll ye have?' we were asked as hands were shaken along with pronouncements as to the most suitable whisky merited by this auspicious occasion. The Gurkhas's requests (lager or coke) were as modest as their demeanour but a place was cleared for us at the bar, where every passing islander could thump us in congratulation to the point where large-scale bruising was a dead cert. On the plus side, we couldn't buy ourselves a drink.

'Where have ye walked from the day?' asked one.

'Er, what's it called, Neil? Barra Head?' guessed Dhal.

'Barra Head, the day?' gasped the Lewisman, his eyes blinking in astonishment.

'No, the Butt of Lewis!' Ewen corrected.

'Aha! Didnae think youse boys could fly as well!' he laughed.

'A good march though,' put in another. 'We call it Gige Chaluim, Calum's gig, what you'd call Shanks pony.' Most were speaking in English but not all.

'Shanks pony?' asked Dhal blankly.

'Oh, aye,' the Gaelic-speaker said, quickly realising that he wasn't from the only group to have English as a second language. 'Your feet,' he explained, rather over-doing it by pointing and making an exaggerated mime of walking.

We had all been entertained here the night before when the Club had officially opened a refurbished wing, The Highlander Suite, but we were just off the ferry and in transit to our accommodation in Harris. Consequently, we had left as early as was politely possible but the

Legionnaires had taken their celebratory duties so seriously that the new suite was busy until way past midnight. The same crowd had returned to finish the job properly at lunchtime today, though in the normal bar.

'Hey, Neil, we've put a big collection bottle for ye on the bar. We'll open it up later and send on the cash!' called the barman. 'It's raised tens of pounds already.' It was flattering that so many knew my name, but it was equally embarrassing that I did not know theirs. So many were called 'Lachie' that I began to suspect this was a wind-up. 'Right, thanks, Lachie,' I hooted back. Three heads turned.

There would be, I surmised, the economy size, no frills Lachie, then Big Lachie and not forgetting Wee Lachie before we got to the big puddin' himsel' Lachie of Lachie of that ilk. 'Lachie Come Home,' I giggled to myself. We had just hammered twenty-six miles and part of my mind was out of control with fatigue, but even so I knew that this was not the wisest place to start making Lachie jokes

After a day of solid marching, I, for one, did not want to spend too long in a bar, no matter how congenial and generous the patrons. I wanted a shower and supper, and could see that the boys were ready to move too.

In the car park our departure was delayed by a pensioner who was knee-walking drunk. 'My grandfather was saved by Gurkhas in the trenches,' he claimed. I presumed that he had met Campbell earlier, as the story began in the middle and it was Campbell he engaged, but when we eventually drove off it transpired that Campbell had never met him before and thought he had been a friend of mine. Hence neither he nor I had hurried him.

Like all soldiers, Gurkhas can fall asleep whenever there is a spare minute and the half-hour drive back to Tarbert saw them drop off immediately. This was a mistake as we were travelling through some of the most extraordinary landscapes in the world. While we sped past the flat boglands of Lewis and its thousand reed-rimmed ponds, ahead grew the stony shoulders of Harris.

Lewis and Harris are geographically a single unit yet are as topographically divided as it's possible to be. Though both share the same metamorphic rock, beyond that everything else is different. The north lies in what was Ross-shire while the south was Inverness-shire, and the abrupt change from water-logged tarn-dotted Lewis to grey mountain is astonishing. Faulting and uplift created Harris, while glaciation and frost splintered and polished its elephantine folds. Grain and strata present themselves as if for a kid's geology lesson and there is barely a spot of green, giving it the bald barren look of badlands, brigandage and desolation. Drowned valleys indent the coast with long meandering fjords. Loch Seaforth, for instance, is eighteen miles long and drops to 325 feet.

There is something ageless and immovable about mountains, especially exposed rock, as if scraped down to the bone, like here in Harris. We have few words to describe anything bigger than a mountain and their immutability reminds us of the transience of life. Particularly these ones. Lewisian gneiss is the world's oldest stone, created 3,000 million years ago (Ayer's Rock is a mere 100 million years old), and while Lewis itself has been ground down like old molars, Harris still rears its rocky head into the Atlantic skies. This is the oldest fragment of Europe and we were at its top edge. The Hebrides begin the world's tale and our little van was crossing the earliest foundations of Creation.

The route curved up to the skyline through a sweeping series of switchbacks where first there was the ubiquitous bog and then simply boulder, grit and grey sheet rock as if greenery were not permitted. This dramatic change took place over a few hundred yards and in the back of our van Suk and Nugendra opened their eyes to take in the extraordinary landscape. But there were no words, only fascination and murmurs of admiration. The boys from the Himalaya were at home in Harris.

'We'll meet up for supper at 8.30,' I announced as the Caravelle drew up outside Tarbert's Harris Hotel. 'Ram, khursani remember, you're in charge of the khursani,' I said, referring to the chilli peppers that were an essential accompaniment for every Gurkha meal and were stored in the back of the van. We had brought a football and the guys were booting it about as if this were playtime. In contrast, I dragged my pack over to the hotel, amid the usual end-of-school high spirits of the others, and headed for a shower, keen to hit the hot water before my knees locked in the sitting position – which would be more than mildly embarrassing for someone who saw himself, in the heroic mould, as a great leader of mountain men. Only humility ever prevents me from actually saying so, of course.

When we found ourselves tucked round a table in the neatly comfortable dining room, the whole team was unthinkingly still in blue polo shirts under light grey sweat shirts as if declaring their pride in our group identity. The crossed kukris embroidered on the left breast above the words 'Hebridean Gurkha' was a smart badge to wear too. The room was full of mostly Scottish and English pensioners who smiled gently in our direction.

'Can we have what we want?' asked Suk, looking over the menu with such a big smile it seemed he was ready to order every single item. 'Have what you want. I think we're all starving, aren't we?' There was a hearty cackle of agreement as eyes looked down. Dhal had his work cut out as interpreter because there was hardly a dish that his colleagues understood. Both Nugendra and Suk were keen to improve their English but, as infantrymen, they worked alongside mostly other Gurkhas and the opportunity was limited. Soon our orders were delivered; steak was the favourite.

The Harris Hotel is a wee gem and there were heaps of good quality vegetables, including big bowls of chips or mashed potato. I had specifically warned the chef that the boys had to have rice and there were mounds of this too. To my surprise the lads loaded up their plates with chips, potatoes and rice. I had forgotten just how much food can be packed away by young soldiers.

But before picking up the cutlery everyone started looking at the table as if searching for something and then looking enquiringly at each other. 'Ramkumar, khursani?' I asked. There was an explosion of self-admonishment as Ram jumped from the table. 'Ram! The keys!' shouted Campbell, tossing them over. Within moments the miscreant i/c chilli was back bearing several types of red and green, thin and fat khursani.

Now the feast could begin! We had discovered from past Gurkha marches how important it was for team-bonding to eat together and the lesson was reaffirmed as the heroic warriors swapped war stories about today's magnificent campaign over plates piled so high we had to eat quickly to prevent our meals toppling on to the tablecloth.

'Tomorrow we attack here?' asked Suk.

'Well, we walk from Stornoway to here,' I replied, knowing he meant the hotel would be the target. 'You've seen the road.'

'So, no crisis of leadership?' asked Ewen.

'Well, I was a bit worried about all that unending road,' I replied shrugging.

The proprietor was one of the many islanders to have made a donation in answer to our pre-march adverts (many had told us they'd keep 'the kettle on') and came over to say hello. The boys, of course, behaved like perfect gentlemen, as indeed they always do. How is it, I wondered, that the most polite cheerful folk on the planet are also a bye-word for military ferocity? The conundrum lies waiting to be answered. I only know it exists and am very happy they're on our side.

Having ruthlessly attacked all the wonders delivered to our table, we retired for coffee in an adjacent lounge. Our assault on the chocolates was unstoppable, but the Terry's of York had been deployed in a particularly provocative way and our self-control evaporated. For once, we all lost our heads.

Tightening tendons and a happy drowsiness saw me stumbling to the room I shared with Dhal. There was a strange presence in the bathroom, a figure neither benign nor malign. I could sense it even when in my bed next door. 'Oh, great,' I thought, 'I've become all fey too.' I didn't mention it to anyone, it didn't seem worth it, and fell fast asleep.

CHAPTER TWO

STORNOWAY TO TARBERT

Walking from the most northerly point of the Outer Isles to the most southerly had seemed a good idea once upon a time. A smug friend had chided me for ignoring, or being ignorant of, the prevailing wind which would helpfully blow on our backs if we started in the south. But there had never been any question in my mind that we might not go from the top of the map. It was a decision I never regretted. The final push to the islet of Barra Head, by small boat over eighteen miles of sea, would represent a proper culmination of our endeavour whatever the wind's direction. We would plant our flags on its summit with an élan that could not be reproduced on the flatlands of Lewis. The walking wouldn't be back breaking and with Gurkhas stationed in Edinburgh for the first time ever, the travel arrangements would be both simple and cheap. The Hebrides are a magical place of lore and beauty whose call I'd heard first as a dreamy whisper. I can't even remember when. Before I knew it, we were off.

This year, instead of every soldier travelling from the far south of England, Campbell and I had merely picked them up from their barracks in south Edinburgh. The four of them stood in smart casual wear outside the guardroom in bright expectation, the two big guys and the two wee ones, as I gave a stumbling half-English, half-Nepali, description of what we were planning.

'So we are going today?' asked Suk.

'We are leaving Edinburgh tomorrow morning, but you are all leaving the barracks with me now,' I explained, half puzzled. This was not exactly an unimportant detail. How come the team didn't seem to know that this was the day of departure? This had happened to me before with Gurkhas when one group had blithely turned up a day early but hadn't seen fit to even ring and warn me.

We all strolled over to the Company Orderly Room to pick up their bags and to make sure with the Company Sergeant Major that all sides, including his, knew when we were going. Gurkhas are famously unimpressed with clocks, and like the Islanders, prefer to be governed by the sun, moon and – best of all – the seasons.

The sergeant major grinned slowly when he discovered my concern, as if encountering an old but faintly amusing problem. 'Ah boys, boys!' he smiled before rattling off in Nepali that they were to leave now. This apparently was a repeat performance of the instructions he had delivered not an hour ago. Within minutes we were heading north to my office to pick up some gear and have lunch. The fifth member of the team, our Senior NCO, Sergeant Dhal, then appeared, having taken the train from his base near Nuneaton. The reunion with fellow piper Ram was a noisy affair but Gurkhas are always pleased to meet colleagues and the others seemed only marginally less delighted.

Though they already had blue rain jerkins, blue polo shirts, baseball caps and grey sweat shirts complete with the crossed kukri emblem, more gear was necessary and we headed off to an outdoor shop in town to buy it.

Milletts in Frederick Street had been warned about our arrival and a hefty discount had been negotiated. I'd been heavy in my hints that I nearly represented over a hundred city-based Gurkhas and the staff was correspondingly eager. Boots were eschewed for strongly-built trainers. Knapsacks and shorts were snapped up, though Kesh and Ram ended up with ladies' shorts. Aware that shoe size six and under are classed as

Overleaf. ***Left:*** **Loch Broom. See the seal?**
Right: **The boys enjoying the sun at Ullapool.**

children's clothes, and thus exempt from VAT, I was only miffed to discover everyone's feet began at size seven. Nugendra was sitting next to a heap of heavy-duty socks.

'Yo topaiko ho?' Is this yours? I asked.

He nodded. 'You're only to have four pairs, you know,' I said.

'I heard you say twenty,' he replied thoughtfully.

'Twenty? We're only walking for a week! Twenty for all of us maybe.'

Flustered, the big Gurung tried to laugh it off but was obviously embarrassed at both his stupidity and apparent attempt to grab a truckload of socks.

There was time for a trip to Tesco (who gave us a discount) to buy fruit and chocolate, plus armfuls of the vital khursani. I don't think my loyalty card ever received so many points.

When it came to kip down in my flat, Nugendra and Suk shared the living room; Suk on the couch and Nugendra on my great aunt's First World War camp bed. 'Ah,' they both exclaimed, unfolding it. 'American camp bed!'

'No, that was used by a nurse in 1914 in Belgium and France,' I replied laughing.

There had been a moment of drama when the entire block was shaken by the shattering volume of both Ram and Dhal opening up with their pipes. Our senses reeled as if under attack. I sprinted through to their room with racing pulse and dilated pupils. The noise hit me with a roar of energy as I flung open the door. The two guys looked up in surprise over sheet music which was laid all over the floor, looking like it had been blasted there. 'Guys! Guys! Not in a flat!' The folk in the next door block were suddenly at their windows, staring inquiringly. It was left to me to explain to Dhal and Ram the anti-social possibilities of playing the great Highland pipe in small civilian housing units, even in the Scottish capital.

By eight the next morning we were on our way, stopping briefly at the pretty Perthshire town of Pitlochry where it took us a while to find anywhere open for bacon rolls and coffee. The van, under grey skies, at last hit the seven-mile-long sea inlet of Loch Broom where at the far end lay the sun-lit buildings of Ullapool, like some fabled journey's end. We had three hours before the ferry sailed. Who said Gurkhas are always late?

Magnificent servings of fish and chips were provided in a seafront beer garden and a rising heat. 'This is the life,' grinned Dhal. The boys, all in dark glasses, sat in a row watching a couple of fishing boats tying up under cloudless skies. 'Look! A, a, a ... ' pointed Suk. A large Atlantic seal appeared alongside the vessels and simply remained there, yawning. 'Probably waiting for scraps,' guessed Campbell.

This was just too interesting and everyone left their seats to check it out. The sleek head turned to inspect the Nepalese visitors but then ignored them, as if waiting for lunch not a group of hooting, whistling, waving spectators.

We wandered round Ullapool, admiring the tree-lined streets with their houses set well back behind neatly cut lawns. The whole town had been designed by a pupil of Thomas Telford after the British Society for Extending the Fisheries had set up a fishing station to take advantage of the herring to be found in Loch Broom. But nature's a funny thing, and in the early years of the nineteenth century the shoals forsook the loch. When the East European Klondykers turned up in the 1970s they were after mackerel and had stripped out the area by the late 1980s.

To our astonishment the group found itself standing outside the village hall which was holding – of all things – a sale of Nepalese goods. Inside two Canadians were manning sales tables of Hindu deities, carved mani stones, Buddhist wall hangings, prints of the Himalaya and racks of jerseys and jackets.

'I'll get this for my mother,' said Suk, holding up a purse.

'You're going to go home from Scotland with a purse for your mum made in Kathmandu?' asked Ewen. 'Don't even think about it!'

Suk nodded and burst out laughing, but returned the purse to the table. Even the Canadians smiled. Nugendra bought a small bust of Shiva while I settled on a string of prayer flags, *dhoza*, for a special occasion I had in mind.

Gurkhas love tartan and every unit lays claim to its own. Suk's Battalion wears Hunting Stewart, while Dhal's Corps, The Queen's

Overleaf. *Left:* Dhal, Ram and Ewen inspect the ferry.
***Right:* Looking back across the Minch. Ullapool is hidden on right.**

Gurkha Signals have Grant, while Ram, as an infantry piper, would wear Douglas tartan trews. Gifts for the family, if possible, had to be in tartan of some sort – be they purses, wallets or spectacle cases. There are countless photos of mothers sitting on their forecourt in Nepal, clad in a headscarf of the check cloth of Scotland. This isn't just affection, it sends out the subtle but proud message that 'my son is in the Gurkhas'.

The van, in hot still sunshine, was, of course, first in the ferry queue, but was quickly joined by a long line of cars and trucks. In no time we were sitting on the top deck, taking in a magnificently blue view of the stretching sea and the surrounding tousled landscape. To our north was a panorama of rising and falling hills so immense it captured the perspective of a Chinese print. The wind rose as we entered the Minch but only the smallest waves broke round about, their backs ice-cream white which only deepened the blue of the sea.

In the hey day of MacBrayne's each of their steamers had a dining saloon with snowy linen and heavy cutlery, but today we were presented with only a cafeteria in which sat lonely fat schoolchildren comfort-eating their way through pizzas and orange-brown fried food. This was late Friday afternoon. Ewen asked aloud: 'Perhaps they're going home from school?'

'Hmm, dunno. Stornoway has a very good secondary school, the Nicholson Institute.' I offered.

'Can't be, this is July,' added Campbell, a father who knows all about these things.

'And anyway, don't they ban Sunday sailings? The kids would have to miss most of Monday morning to go to school on the mainland.'

Sabbatarianism taken to extremes is a fairly modern innovation in the Outer Hebrides. The steamers used to sail on Sundays until a 1930s' petition. In the 1960s the Church had a complete victory on Sunday flying and in the 1970s land at Arnish, beside the harbour, was only leased by the Stornoway Trust to Fred Olsen on condition of no Sunday working at his fabrication yard. For years there was a famous photo of children's swings padlocked together depicting, allegedly, a Hebridean Sabbath that accompanied any article in the Scottish press describing the vexed question of Sabbatarianism – despite every photographer in the land knowing the picture to be a fake.

'Perhaps they could fly El Al?'

Conversations like this completely lost our Gurkha pals, even though they would listen with interest and even smile at the appropriate moment. Mind you, some of the religious goings-on in the Isles would confuse any outsider. We sat pulling faces over watery coffee, as the low pale shape of Lewis came into focus in the West.

'Do you speak Hindi, Neil?' asked Nugendra.

'No.'

'I enjoy speaking Hindi very much,' he replied.

'Where did you learn?'

'Bharat, India, my father was Gurkha in Indian Army.'

A light suddenly went on in my head. The only other tall Gurkha I knew was a Limbu called Rabindra – and his father had been in the Indian Army. Of course! He'd have had a good childhood diet. Gurkhas are not genetically small; they are merely proof that you cannot bring up strapping six-footers on lentils.

'Do you know Rabindrakumar Jabegu?' I asked.

There was a big flash of white teeth. 'We were in the same intake!'

It became obvious that we were in the middle of a huge NATO exercise with silhouetted destroyers and jets moving slowly across the horizon, while occasionally we were over-flown by helicopters complete with anti-submarine domes. As we stood lining a shiprail, a group of Royal Navy sailors gave us a once-over as if wondering what the heck a small group of undercover Gurkhas was doing in the exercise area. Greetings were exchanged but no information!

A Lewisman grinned that the military activity around the harbour mouth probably centred on the fact that the seabed dropped suddenly by about 200 feet only a half mile from the quayside where, in his opinion, a sub was probably at this moment skulking.

The fifty-mile sea journey completed in utter peace, we drove round to the British Legion's premises where there was a welcoming line of office bearers on the pavement as if we were visiting royalty. Flash guns flickered, a piper blew and I was left shaking hands with the town's unco guid while introducing my awestruck gang. A couple of journalists quizzed me as to the trip – we got good ensuing coverage – but there was a couple of clever-dick questions concerning fundraising treks on the Sabbath which I had to deal with carefully. For instance, did 'We're doing God's work' sound facetious?

There was time for a couple of pints to mark the opening of the new suite and then we were away to our hotel at Tarbert in Harris.

Two days later we were in Stornoway for our third and last time to begin Day Two's march, the route south to the hotel. The town's name is Norse for 'Bay of the Anchor' and has a correspondingly long history. James VI had been concerned that the rents due by the Macleods of Lewis were long overdue and had heard that their people had 'given themselves over to all kind of barbaritie and inhumanitie', meaning his royal authority had to be asserted. Reports suggested that the Isle was something of an El Dorado too. It was 'inrychit with ane increibill fertilietie of cornis and store of fischeingis and utheris necessaries, surpassing far the plenty of any pairt of the inland.' The mugs that followed this up were a body of gentlemen, largely from Fife, known as 'The Fife Adventurers' and drew up a contract with the King in 1598 to take advantage of this veritable promised land, which included the 'ruiting out the barbarous inhabitantis'.

The Macleods gave them a stiff welcome but the Adventurers managed to gain a foothold in Stornoway and build a fortification. But food ran short. Believing that Lewis was flowing with milk and honey, they had naïvely neglected to bring stores with them. Led by Chief Neil Macleod with 'two hundred barbarius, bludie and wicket Hielandmen' the locals killed twenty-two of the camp and made off with the horses and sheep. Neil Macleod then joined the Adventurers, and was instrumental in the treacherous capture of his brother Murdoch. Twelve followers were beheaded and the heads sent in a sack to Edinburgh. Neil then turned on his new allies who fled. The charter was later sold to Kenneth Mackenzie of Kintail (descendants became Lord Seaforth), a mainland clan which remained in control until the 19th Century. Not the sort of place to start a fight then.

The fable of the Isles' natural riches was not new, going as far back as the Vikings. One Norse saga refers to a raid in 800 A.D. when 'fire played in the fig trees of Lewis'. We might take this as the birth of Hebridean poetic licence and their tradition of story-telling in its broadest sense.

At the time of the Commonwealth, Stornoway was occupied by English Roundheads under a Colonel Cobbet – who must have offended someone pretty important – and it is the Puritans' fanaticism for the letter of the law that pervades the famous Lewis Coffee Shop sugar scandal of 1918 when said establishment was fined £3 for having shamelessly served two individuals – and contravened the Public Meals order – with cups of tea and sugar. The individuals plead guilty but were loud in their assertion that they expected tea to be served with sugar in a café. 'Not so,' quoth Sheriff Dunbar. 'You must understand you are not entitled to sugar anywhere, except your own ration.' If they came again, they must bring their own sugar. Being a first offence, the sheriff imposed a lenient ten shillings fine or a heck-I'm-feeling-generous-today five days imprisonment. The island authorities, normally outsiders, always had such a manic regard for order among their subordinates. Frankly, I'm only surprised that they weren't done for wilful tea consumption outwith the appropriate legislation too.

Today, with flasks replete with sweet tea, the Hebridean Gurkhas began walking from the town's entrance at a hearty pace which I hoped merely reflected a morning freshness that would quickly settle down to something more sensible. The tarmac lolloped ahead, like a kid's painting of a road which rose and fell to the distant hills of Harris which were half hidden under rain clouds. Concerned for my knees, particularly the left one, I had had them checked by a friend who is qualified in sports medicine. Her verdict? 'There's nothing wrong with your left knee, except a bit of cripitis – the shin muscle that attaches to the knee is slightly ripped – but it will heal. Your right knee, though, needs surgery!' Altogether now: we've amputated the wrong leg but the good news is that the other one's getting better.

I had come across cripitis long ago when I asked a paratrooper in Northern Ireland why he was limping. He gave me an embarrassed look

Overleaf. ***Left*****: The hills of Harris in the background are rain-covered but the road to Tarbert is sunny.**
Right: **Typical road scene – a ribbon of tarmac to the horizon.**

before confiding: 'Cystitis.'

'Really?' I marvelled. 'Trust the Paras!'

'Wha' yer sayin'?' he warned, baffled but aggressive.

I later learned he meant cripitis. Not surprisingly, I was never going to forget the word.

Day Two was the Sabbath and the two-lane road was mostly empty. Black clouds seemed trapped over Harris but a gentle sun lit our route as if we were in some celestial spotlight. To our left and right the sky was downright busy but we seemed blessed. Dhal was with us again and miles were being clocked off with an unremitting energy that seemed contagious for the moment.

There had been concern when Ram was asked at the British Legion if he'd been here before. His reply – 'Yes, Belfast' – implied that the boys weren't altogether certain as to exactly where they were. It's long been a criticism of the Gurkhas that they tend to show little interest in 'abroad' – just like British soldiers – but Scotland is normally different. The shared pipes, tartan, mountains, martial tradition and love of drink and dance, mean that there is a special link between our two countries. Claymores, dirks or kukris, they're all from the same family.

'Do you like Edinburgh?' I asked Suk.

'Yes, good posting,' he replied before looking rueful and adding, 'But expensive.' Ah, yes. The temptation to go drinking or buy flash clothes and gadgets always hovered outside the camp gate. This nixed the whole point of being in the Gurkhas: to make and save the type of money that will transform their lives once back in Nepal. Blowing it every week in Edinburgh is not part of the plan but is an undeniable fact of life. Suk was practically a walking advert of its dangers.

'Whenever you look at a map of Britain, you know, you'll see these Isles and say "I walked from up there to down there,"' I said. The nods in reply seemed uncertain and again I wondered: do they know where they are? Gurkhas are rarely seen here; perhaps we're the first.

The Stornoway–London distance is the same as London–Czech Republic. At least I knew where I was. Anywhere with 'Outer' in its name implies a certain remoteness but I'd bet a dollar to a rupee that the boys could not interpret the word and merely thought it part of the place name.

The passing scenery of open, pond-ridden moor, where the map of the land to our north was more blue than white, was, to them, just another vista of the UK. Almost everything in their young lives was new but was always accepted without comment, be it internal plumbing, air travel or even the sea. Many had not encountered a motor car until their twenties but they all had e-mail addresses and had a better grasp of IT than me.

All Gurkhas live up to the stereotype: eager, cheerful, courteous and gentle. They are proud to be soldiers and believe in loyalty to the Regiment and friends, in courage, and in giving the best of themselves. They obey readily but retain a refreshing independence of spirit which does not include servility. They will work hard and happily for you, but there must be respect, because they're easily as good as you and you are lucky to have them alongside. In fact, they're all my superior. Every year a chosen 10,000 put themselves forward for selection and are whittled down to just 230. My men had all passed the sternest entrance exam in military history. You will not be shocked to learn that they'd never heard of an inferiority complex.

Today they chattered happily among themselves in their own language. Kesh and Ram hardly spoke English and I worried that I wasn't giving them enough attention but, reassuringly, they met my every look with a merry smile. The team resembled a fast-moving train with Ewen striding out at its front with the lads as sleek carriages and then me as a clunky old-fashioned guard's van in the rear which was never going to be exactly stream-lined but somehow was part of the whole. For a guard's van, I puffed rather too much.

Up ahead Ewen had called a stop and, with Nugendra and Dhal, had flung himself down on the roadside. This was outside a wee cottage and as I walked up, an elderly woman, all in black, complete with black poke bonnet and holding a black-bound bible in both hands, appeared in their midst.

'Dhal, mero sathi, tik chha?' I greeted, wondering what the old lady from Little House on the Prairie was saying. To my surprise, she hadn't said a thing, and stood purse-lipped on the verge between the seated Kesh and Suk, frowning.

'Good morning,' I said. Nothing. No response. As far as she was concerned we didn't exist. She couldn't see us or hear us. Before the situation could develop a glossy car drew up, driven perhaps by her son, and she hurried forward. Not even a look back. It would be untrue to describe this incident as troubling but I couldn't help feeling a touch hurt. This was the first, and as it transpired, the only individual who, instead of meeting the boys with a smile, bristled. For a moment I had toyed with a charming series of introductions to my Buddhist and Hindu friends but (I couldn't help giggling) who would probably be seen as godless heathens. Perhaps I was reading too much into it; the boys seemed oblivious.

Further down the road we passed a church with rows of cars outside. From within came the locked-in sound of singing. Alas, not the keening counter melodies of Gaelic hymns but the normal straightforward English stuff. There were two Gaelic services per Sabbath, we read from the noticeboard, but this was the English one. The lads quietly approved of this religious observance and we tramped on our way feeling great. Though I love the evocative soaring of Gaelic plainsong, I am always aware of how foreign it is, and I realise that I am not of this culture at all.

It is interesting to note that the Norse had been a dominant minority here many centuries ago, and it was here that Christianity began one of its tentative steps into the Dark Ages when its light had nearly been extinguished throughout Europe. The Hebrides used to come under the Bishopric of Trondheim. By the closing years of the 9th century, a famous Hebridean warrior, Helgi the Lean, was known to 'pray to Christ at home but to Thor in a tight corner'.

The Isles are not of the mainland, even genetically. The Macdonalds, for instance, were founded by one Donald, the grandson of Somerled, Lord of the Isles. 'Somerled' means 'summer visitor' i.e. Viking. It was this man, who by building his own warships, overthrew the Norse rulers in 1158, and announced the arrival of a new warrior people, Gall-Gaedhil, Foreign Gael, who spoke Gaelic not Norse. The Gaelic for the Western Isles is Innse Gall, the Islands of Strangers, which reflects their non-Scottish roots.

'Ram, you're married, aren't you?'

'Yes,' he said slowly, as if answering the obvious: 'One daughter.'

'How old?'

'Four months. Born in Edinburgh.'

'Oh, which hospital?'

'Simpson.'

'The same as me!' I laughed, 'As well as half of Edinburgh!'

'What about you, Suk?'

Suk rolled his eyes, grinned and declared: 'I never marry.'

'I bet you will. Next long leave!'

Suk chuckled and shook his head. This was a surprise. All Gurkhas marry young, indeed are expected to and want to. That Ewen and I were single was a frequent source of curiosity.

'You have too many girlfriends!' put in Dhal, referring to me almost critically, but his lean face split by a white smile. As events were to show, this was a case of pots and kettles as I was soon to receive an invitation to Dhal's second wedding. And I was right about Suk; he did come back from his next trip to Nepal as a married man.

'Does your family still live in the home village?'

Suk's face looked momentarily troubled. 'My mother and sister have moved to Kathmandu because of Maoists. The Maoists always want money. Is expensive in Kathmandu. The houses are expensive and on our farm you live without paying for your house.'

The men nodded in silent assent. Their country was being torn apart and their position as Gurkhas, on Western-size salaries, left their families vulnerable to extortion by Peking-backed insurgents. The world didn't seem interested in the nightmare facing the people of Nepal and these guys' families were taking the brunt of it.

Rain began to fall. The inevitable, unheralded rain. Really heavy stuff that poured off the peaks of our caps like shower curtains. Somehow it was so normal that no one bothered. We even found ourselves thumping through a small area of forestry which had earlier intrigued me when examining large scale satellite pictures of the area because our road seemed visible. Visible from 12,000 miles! Surely there was something wrong? After a second or two, I'd guessed that they must have chopped

Overleaf. *Left:* Callanish. Late evening, bright smiles.
***Right:* Dhal. Standing stones; leaning Gurkha.**

back the trees from the road, hence we had sight of a mile-broad track from above the stratosphere. I was childishly delighted that my deduction had been correct. It didn't mean that the walking was any less demanding though and my legs were beginning to ache as if I'd been involved in an accident involving sledge-hammers and my feet were numb. The steady jog-trot, though, remained remorseless.

There was no sign that we had offended the Lord's Day Observance folk. Drivers were now stopping to give us donations. One was a big bag of coins which had been collected at some social gathering. Its weight promised wealth aplenty but we were to be disappointed. It was all small change, but even so it represented a communal will to support us.

The landscape at last began to buckle and climb, and we found ourselves actually inside the swirling clouds of Harris which wrapped themselves round our shoulders like smoky scarves. Soon there was the long finger of Loch Seaforth on our left and I remembered that Bonnie Prince Charlie had sailed up here on 4th May 1746 on the run after the catastrophe of Culloden Moor. His group had then taken thirty-six hours to march the roadless twenty or so miles to Stornoway, arriving outside the town on the 5th May. The Prince's aide, Donal Macleod went ahead and successfully commissioned a ship to sail to France but one of his men had got drunk and blabbed. The good folk of Stornoway feared Government vengeance if the news got out, but their sympathies allowed the Prince to set out the next morning – 6th May – in the same boat that had landed them here at Loch Seaforth and had meantime come round to the port. The thought of falling on my face for thirty-six hours from here to Stornoway in foul weather made my blood curdle. The road might have hammered our feet but without it this march would take weeks not days.

It was at Stornoway that we heard of the only two individuals known to have attempted to betray the Prince on the whole of his five-month flight across the Highlands and Islands: a dastardly father and son act, the Rev Aulay Macaulay and boy, the Rev John (grandfather of the historian Lord Macaulay). They were thwarted by a tenant of Scalpay (an isle just near our hotel) who reminded them that they were breaking the law – the law of Highland hospitality. They withdrew in shame.

In mid-afternoon we found ourselves still alongside the loch but walking down to a jetty where Dhal was lying on his front, arms in a nearby burn, guddling for trout. The laughter told me they were up to something.

'Hey! Neil Saheb, look!' called Dhal, holding up a small fish, its white belly twisting in his hold. Fatigue meant my response was muted but we all grinned. Little did we know it but Dhal's propensity for lifting fish with or without permission would get us into trouble and the papers soon.

The road switched to a long rising left and then drove through the Clisham Hills. Their igneous folds rose like stone whales, their backs wet as if the clouds had been exhaled from rocky blowholes. Clisham, at 799 metres, is not even a Munro (3,000 ft./914 m.) but is a formidable summit and the highest point in the Western Isles. The name comes – as always – from the Norse (Kliffa meaning 'cliff') and represented a substantial way-marker. All my men were from western Nepal and, don't be astonished, hardly noticed the 190 metre climb to reach the top of the pass. The Kagmara, just to the West of Suk's home village, is one of the highest passes in the world, and rises to 5,400 metres. Even in Nepal this is considered high. Kagmara means 'The Pass Where Jackdaws Die'. Charmingly, altitude sickness has given its name to two nearby ranges: the Headache Mountains and the Little Headache Mountains.

The final few miles through low wet cloud and dripping stone saw us like ants crossing a glistening rockery, but morale – that strange word – was blazing on about Gas Mark 7 when we warmly greeted our hotel at Tarbert. It had been a weary but necessary journey; no one had learned much but another road Marathon had been completed and we were happy for that. We knew what we'd accomplished, and the most featureless sections of our task were now behind us. From now on we'd really see island magic; big white beaches and machair full of wild flowers.

Supper was another feast. If there were a programme called, say, Monster Portions TV, we'd be the hands-down winners. Standing up post meal, I nearly keeled over as my legs stiffly refused to obey the command

Overleaf. *Left:* See the Stones at Lewis? Older than Mick and Keith.
***Right:* Callanish. Memorial in stone to a lost past.**

to leave. 'God, I feel like Douglas Bader,' I winced to the couple alongside. There was a roar of laughter from fellow diners; the couple were German. There had been a pre-prandial stushie when it was discovered that two English men in the bar were not residents, and therefore not legally permitted to order the drinks they were already sipping. Both sides seemed deeply apologetic; the English didn't want to cause offence and the barmaid didn't want to impose the restriction but knew her job was on the line if she didn't. We all shook our heads.

After the meal, with the sun up nearly all night hereabouts, we were far from finished. The fifty-six Standing Stones at Callanish are 5,000 years old and pre-date the Pyramids of Giza and Stonehenge by half a millennium. No one's really sure what they were for, but one thing's certain; they are stunning reminders of a lost past. Spaced in a cross shape with a group in a circle at its centre, they stand like a platoon of ten-foot sentinels overlooking the Atlantic sea loch, Loch Roag, on south-west Lewis. Everyone was keen and curious to visit.

On arrival, we waited a moment as a film crew shot the monoliths in the grey evening light, made evocative by a gentle breeze. Events were being held up by a border collie that saw himself as auditioning for the next *Lassie* movie and would cheerfully potter over to centre stage, sit, grin at camera and patiently await direction. Of course, the crew was tearing its hair out and the soundman was manically trying to distract the dog while at the same time fiddling with his fluffy boom mike and chest of wee dials. When we turned up, there was an air of frustrated hopelessness: more people to spoil the picture. But Suk and Ram simply grabbed the collie by its neck and sat with it out of camera.

'Thanks, guys,' exhaled the director. Their task took minutes and they were quickly gone. Suk produced a jack knife and cut free the dog's collar of tangled baling twine, and now had a friend for life. The owner, though, would doubtless spend the evening wondering how his collie had removed the mess.

'These are very good,' murmured Nugendra. All the men stroked the pale grey stones as if communing and seemed wonder-stuck by every one of them. There were many more in the surrounding peat. In fact, we had been initially confused and nearly pulled up in front of the wrong ones.

Again, I was aware that there was deep approval for things spiritual (if indeed the Stones were that). Nepal shares a tradition with Scotland of ancient stone symbols. Throughout the Himalaya, stones are carved with Buddhist tracts and whole walls of sacred tablets have been built over the millennia. Stone survives beyond even the message, as Callanish proves. They hid a mystery but then the Gods are beyond understanding anyway, and the Stones' enigma seemed only appropriate. They had only been re-discovered by Sir James Matheson in 1857 when they were dug out of five feet of peat. To me they spoke of an ancient brooding wish to reach for something untouchable. They were as clean as if erected last month.

There's only one conclusion we can make about Callanish, and it's a surprising one: that Neolithic islanders were so wealthy that they had time to indulge in massive engineering projects. Though we took a ton of photos, Suk later wanted all mine too. The monoliths had made an impression deeper than I had realised. 'We saw the Stones in Lewis' has a great ring to it – even though most would assume we meant Mick and Keith. As we headed back to Tarbert, it crossed my mind that we were leaving Lewis for the last time.

The following Christmas there was one of those 'All Right on the Night' TV programmes presented by Denis Norden. There on the screen was our little Callanish scene and, lo and behold, our laughing collie, complete with noises from the crew. A shot of Gurkhas coming to the rescue would have made a good, if surprising, climax but it was not to be. We'd nearly made network TV!

On a shore ten miles to our west, one Malcolm Macleod was crossing the dunes in 1831 when the ground gave way beneath his feet and, horrified, he watched as a host of small angry figures emerged from the soft shifting sand. Convinced he'd accidentally chanced upon the Kingdom of the Fairies, and witnessed elves and goblins, he fled in terror. Malcolm had discovered the Lewis chessmen. There were 91 pieces belonging to at least eight incomplete sets. Carved from walrus ivory in the twelfth century of Scandinavian design, they are now a Scottish totem – though none today are, controversially, to be found in Lewis. They feature the first ever depiction of a bishop and the rook is represented by a shield-chewing Berserker, or Lead-Biter, the frenzied Norse warrior of myth. Ledbitter is still a surname in the Northern Isles.

So, Vikings wiled away the long northern evenings by developing classic chess moves? This is terrible PR for the boys and severely damages the brand. Hardly rock and rock, is it? Where's the rape and pillage? Of course, these were the men who created the original saga holidays.

There seemed not an acre of these Isles that didn't have a story to tell. My Gurkha pals loved the tales of warriors, fairy stories, and especially underdogs who outwitted wicked overlords. Folk beliefs were always listened to with interest but, frankly, anything with a wee bit of gore went down a treat.

'Tell us the story of the sea woman, Neil,' asked Nugendra, as we later sat drinking tea, 'And we will tell the story of the madal' – the drum. I rattled off a story I'd learned as a kid but was enchanted by the swap. Once a lama, a Brahman and two Gurung shamans had a contest to see who was the most powerful. The losers would burn their books and cut their drums in half. The contest consisted of a race to a lake by the next morning. While the lama and Brahman settled to meditate all night, the shamans flew away on their drums as soon as evening came. When dawn arrived the lama and Brahman climbed a ray of the rising sun and reached the lake at the same time as the sunlight. The shamans arrived only a moment later, but they still lost the race. They burned their books and spilt their drums in half. That is why today only one side of the instrument is covered in skin while the lama has a two-sided drum.

Peoples such as Gaels and Gurkhas, with a heritage of oral traditions, do not renounce it quickly.

CHAPTER THREE

TARBERT TO LEVERBURGH

Our introduction to Harris had been through the rounded, rising skull-like hills of the north, but today we were to march through the rocky skeleton lying to the south. Were it not for the rain and lochans it could be described as lunar. The east of South Harris is low undulating stone, a desolate place almost bare of vegetation, while the western seaboard is comparatively fertile and famous for its white shell-sand beaches backed by machair. It was to the East that small holders were forcibly removed from their traditional dwellings on the West during the 19th century. A famous taunt is that the stones of East Harris are so close together that the noses of the sheep have to be sharpened so that they can get at the grass. No burials are possible there, so that the dead had to be carried across the Isle.

The rain was belting down as heavily as we'd known it when we tramped from the hotel. Our waterproofs were splashed and shiny within seconds. There seemed nothing for it but to put our heads down and just take it. The boys, though, seemed in high spirits and simply grinned. Ram

Overleaf. *Left:* The weather is lifting. Suk looks hopefully at camera.
***Right:* Kesh as we approach the Sound of Taransay.**

then surprised me: 'Neil, my ghunda is not good.'

'Your knee?' I asked, with sickening heart. Ghunda was a word I could never say properly but today I suddenly wasn't worried about its pronunciation. 'How bad?'

'Okay, but needs … '

We strapped it up. He didn't seem discomforted and never mentioned it again but I phoned Campbell to buy a proper knee support. As Tarbert is too small for such a stockist, Campbell found himself directed to the local GP who was glad to provide the necessary but asked the name of the patient.

'Ramkumar Bura?' he repeated.

'Yes, he's a Gurkha.'

'Guessed as much. My family and I are just back from working several years in west Nepal. We must invite them round. How about I pop round to see them this evening?'

Our route took us up a long rise in the driving rain, knees going like pumps. The only traffic was Post Office vans which were obliged to visit daily the many local post boxes studded all over the Isles, often on single posts as if a badge designating 'lonely place'. You wondered just how many people hereabouts had a job that kept them quite so busy. Our road wound west across the island and if the morning was cold and wet, our pace was hot as it can be without actually jogging. This was the suicidal 140 paces per minute rate that eats up four miles an hour and cannot be sustained by the likes of me for very long.

Campbell was parked on the top of the pass. 'Hi, guys! You're making good time!' We stopped under the van's raised rear door out of the rain but ironically gulped down pints of water. While the foreground was a tumbled stretch of sodden stony wasteland, we could clearly see over in the East a war ship which suggested the weather might be lifting.

The group found itself cantering down to the Atlantic, the Sound of Taransay, and under clearing skies. Even in this light, the sea was a beautiful aquamarine and the immense shore a startling white. This was the Hebrides we'd come to see. As the rain stopped, so did we, and the thermos was pulled out. Alongside us a dammed burn had formed a salmon pool which had an angler and ghillie fishing its waters. Given the view, we didn't pay them much attention.

'Hiya, guys!' came an American voice. We looked up to see the ghillie and angler. 'I'm Frank B. Porter Junior, attorney at law. How ya doin'?'

Trying not to laugh, I introduced the gang and explained our trek. It transpired that the ghillie, Gordon Cumming, was the estate factor and knew who we were, not least because the estate owner, Dr David Horrobin, had sent me a big cheque and asked his staff to look out for us. The American was thrilled to meet Gurkhas, especially as he was also the Vice President of the Boston Athletic Association and responsible for the city's Marathon. 'You guys oughta take part! Here,' he said, drawing out his wallet with a flourish. It was stuffed with bank notes. Was he going to pay their airfare? Two of his business cards were generously thrust forward. I've still got them. How do you think I remember all his details?

Over his shoulder, there was a flash of silver. It was Dhal at the poolside landing a big glittering salmon on a handline. 'Oi!' howled Gordon Cumming: 'Put-that-back!' before running down to the pool's edge with steam nearly coming from both ears. Dhal was shaking with laughter and quickly returned the fish. For a couple of minutes both Gurkha and factor stood together, occasionally pointing at the water and obviously swapping happy fish stories.

'I only tried it once!' Dhal explained, climbing up to where we sat. 'I think he's calmed down.'

After a few minutes we were on our way. Today was a journey of just over twenty miles and we'd already covered nine. By teatime we'd be at Leverburgh, the port on the Isle's southern tip and our departure point tomorrow. Day 3 was to be softer on the feet, compared to Day 2's twenty-eight miles – and much easier on the eye.

Just across the Sound lay Taransay, the islet that had starred in Castaway, a TV series that featured a group of volunteers living on it for a year. Remember? Ben Fogle made his name there. I wonder if any ever went back. The 'ay' ending is Norse for 'rocky isle', while 'Taran' is a

Overleaf. *Left:* Shieling with door 'locked' by baling twine.
***Right:* Another Shieling. No Georgian coach lamps here.**

Viking name. The 's', like German and English, indicates the possessive.

The sun suddenly burst through, illuminating the sea from above. The shafts hit the pale seabed below, flooding it with light, in a dazzling dance of turquoise. The huge beach lit up with a blinding glare too. The moment was so uplifting that everyone stopped to photograph it. The same shot appears in countless calendars and brochures but nothing approaches the exhilaration of seeing it in person – and we had somehow witnessed God's scene-shifters transforming it from exceptional to utterly glorious.

The machair was about a hundred yards deep but consisted of short grass, not flowers. Behind it there were occasional cottages but more common were shielings. These small dwellings had not come from some self-assembly designers based in Stockholm but were the products of local ingenuity with a splendid disregard for nancy-boy features such as properly fitting windows. Front doors were 'locked' by baling twine between handle and nearby fence post. Nobody seemed to actually live in them and ragged tups nibbled on the nettles and dock leaves roundabout. The liberal use of corrugated iron for walls and roofs was reminiscent of the zinc houses of pioneers in, say, Saskatchewan. This should not be too surprising, it's where many of the emigrants left for over the past hundred and fifty years.

Out of the blue a van drew up and a wee man jumped out, announcing that he was Grampian Television. This was Iain MacIver who wanted some shots of us en route, then at our finish at Leverburgh, plus a couple of interviews. No problem. The cameraman took some close-ups of our marching feet and then drove ahead for some long shots. In the midst of what we imagined to be the establishing shot, with us doughty figures heroically emerging from the sweeping landscape, Suk stopped to pee on the roadside. Nugendra hauled him back with admonishments and waves at camera. 'Suk!' Kesh shook his head.

The MacIver family of Lewis in their early days ran a petty smack from Stornoway to Campbeltown. Later, brothers David and Charles operated steamships across the Atlantic. It was stretching coincidence, but their American partner, Sam Cunard, had a surname reflecting the Gaelic words, Cuan Ard, High Seas.

'We'll put this out tomorrow,' explained Iain when we arrived at the camera's position. 'The boys all look hell of a fit!' he added (diplomatically avoiding mention of how I managed to limp with both feet). Clearly a Gurkha supporter, he was delighted to meet everyone.

'I'll get Dhal to welcome us in to Leverburgh with his pipes, if you like?' I asked.

'Yeah, great. We'll see if we can't rustle up a small crowd to welcome you too.'

'Aye right, try Central Casting, Leverburgh branch.'

Knowing Dhal needed a break and that it would make sense to get him picked up now and then dropped at the finish, I phoned Campbell who arrived about fifteen minutes later. All our feet were burning, even Nugendra seemed in pain.

'You okay, Nugenda?'

He gave a slow-motion grimace. 'You can take an early break today if you like. Just hop in the van with Dhal.' But he wasn't having any of it; he wanted to be with us on the march in. Ram's earlier problem now didn't exist either.

The encounter with television reminded me to call *The Scotsman*'s diarist, Simon Pia, in Edinburgh. I sat down on the verge and dialled, always grateful that mobile phones had been invented.

'Hi, Neil, how's it going?'

'The place is extraordinarily beautiful but, you know, alongside every road we've walked has been a ditch full of litter with cans and bottles every few yards. We're on Harris right now and it's the same, cans, bottles wrappers all along the roadside. Then there's dumped cars all over the place … '

'Hold on, Neil, hold on,' interrupted Simon: 'We can't have you slagging off the Hebrides! At least, not until after you've got the money and are back on the mainland!'

We spoke about the boys muddling Northern Ireland with the Northern Isles but Simon was much more interested in the current Hebridean scandal concerning hedgehogs. Several years ago these

Overleaf. *Left:* The Sound of Taransay. Note two small figures on right.
***Right:* Ram and Nugendra take a rest with Taransay backdrop.**

animals had been introduced to the Isles and there was now an extraordinary 5,000 pairs. This represented a fearful threat to eggs of the indigenous bird population which, in the absence of trees, nested on the ground. Conservation groups had planned a hedgehog cull, but hedgehog protection groups had howled protest. At the moment there was an impasse. Simon's eventual piece led on my muddling up loro with lauro but asked why the Gurkhas couldn't carry out the cull with their kukris, being in situ and experts at tracking down reclusive targets over rough terrain.

The Outer Hebrides has an easily upset ecosystem. There are no moles, amphibians, or snakes (except slow-worm) and when in the 1960s some fool allowed mink to escape from a fur farm near Stornoway, they nearly exterminated the rat population. Not such a bad thing, you may think, but they went on to decimate the poultry stock too which is why no crofter today keeps chickens. There remain about 130 pairs of mink on the Isles, and if you're a feathered ground-breeder, they represent a termination threat too.

I put away my phone wondering why the common toad has the strange zoological double name *bufo bufo*, like the corncrake *crex crex*. Can I let you into a wee secret? I am (does it need saying?) a bit of a Latin lover. Or do you smell a *ratus ratus*?

Looking round, I realised that I was alone. Ewen and Suk had removed their boots and socks and were paddling in the glass-clear sea. 'Neil, this is fantastic!' called my brother, 'Cold but great on the feet.' Within seconds I was up to my knees in the water, scrunching the white sand between toes, and the whole team joined in like some big healthy family on a bank holiday that had been mysteriously taken in the Caribbean.

Suk took a hearty mouthful of the water and spat it out immediately. 'It's salt!' he exclaimed. Given that Nepal is a country entirely without salt, it seemed perverse to discover that it was flowing here like, er, water.

'You must know that the sea's salty?' asked Ewen.

Suk nodded blankly. The Gurkha look, meaning he didn't.

'You've been in the sea before, haven't you'

'Brunei, yes, but I didn't think this was salty too. Where does it all come from?'

He had us there.

The road took us further south before turning left. Following the coast to the port, and passing a number of grass-covered lazy beds, feannagan. These raised features are perhaps the most inappropriately named items in agriculture, ever. They represent a back-breaking attempt to wrest a living from a difficult environment. Formed by digging two parallel trenches about six feet apart, the spoil was heaped between them, which would be fertilized with manure and seaweed; their height gave them good drainage too. Every single one of our boys understood their purpose in a moment. Their own land is cultivated in a series of hard-won terraces in which puny crops are forced from the thin soil by hard work.

While the Hebridean Gurkha existence couldn't compare to the daily run of those who once lived here, having clattered twenty miles I was approaching exhaustion. We'd marched seventy-five miles in three days on tarmac and I was feeling it.

'Hello! Hello! This is for you!' trilled an attractive woman, running up behind us, holding a fiver. 'It would have been more but our B&B has had a bad summer.' It's not often pretty women chase me down the street offering cash, and I savoured the moment.

Campbell was waiting at the entrance sign to Leverburgh. I had decided that this was where we would stop but Campbell broke the bad news that the film crew was waiting about three miles down the road at the slipway. I swore violently. It wasn't Campbell's fault but I was nearly at the end of my tether.

'This looks like Port Stanley,' said Suk, taking in the low buildings, heavy on painted corrugated iron. I hadn't realised that Suk had been in the Falklands, but he was right. We had a long walk, culminating in rounding a large loch. Folk came from the well-spaced houses to greet us and thrust cash on us. It was as well we'd walked this last bit after all. The sun was now lighting up the scene and my spirits lifted slightly. There had, of course, been not so much as a down-turned mouth when the boys heard

Overleaf. *Left:* Dhal frowns in the bright light of a sunlit beach.
***Right:* Ewen's calves look healthy but compare them to Suk's.**

we faced an unexpected three miles.

'This town was once owned by Lord Leverhulme, hence the name,' explained Ewen. 'He was a millionaire who owned the whole of Lewis and Harris. Look! That's Lever Hall!'

The history of this area is one of the strangest in Britain. While Harris had stayed in the hands of the Macleod of Dunvegan in Skye, Lewis had been held by Mackenzie of Kintail, who been ennobled as Lord Seaforth in 1797. In 1844 Lewis was sold to Sir James Matheson for £190,000 and immediately faced crop failure and famine. He made his money from selling opium to China, and was to spend a total of £574,000 on his estate, which, no matter how you look at it, represents a hell of a lot of opium. Together with the Highland Relief Board, he improved Stornoway harbour and built the road network. The Western Isles' population had soared by 50% between 1750 and 1810, reaching 55,000 by 1841, creating a terrible land hunger (the current population is 26,600). In 1802 eleven ships carried 3,300 passengers away from the Hebrides. By 1803, twenty thousand were preparing to flee to America when the Passenger Vessels Act put a legal limit on the number of passengers to be carried on various ships. This had the effect of raising the fare from £4 to £10, too high for most. These recommendations were made by Thomas Telford, the great engineer, who had been sent north to find ways of discouraging emigration. The law was abandoned in 1827 when the Government decided that it wanted the area emptied. Officials were disturbed that the emigrants looked healthy and strong, but these were the middle-ranking crofters. The old needed them to stay but the young had to go. James Matheson's improvements included eviction, but when he died his daughter proved equally ruthless.

In 1918 there began an extraordinary and costly experiment when Lord Leverhulme, the Lancashire industrialist, bought both Lewis and Harris, and as sole proprietor of 537,000 acres became the UK's biggest landowner at a stroke. He also inherited much of the anger the crofters felt towards the previous owner, Lady Matheson. Undeterred, the new man, whom the islanders called Bodach An t-Siabain (Old Soap Man), started schemes to change the face of his new possession which were to cost him £200,000 p.a. The plan was to transform the islands by investing massive amounts of his personal fortune to modernise the Isles. An ideal society would be created where assets were properly maximised and the Outer Hebrides could become a place of trade and wealth. He was to face only intransigence. The islanders were not ready to alter their lifestyle so radically, if at all, on the whim of an outsider – a characteristic that holds good today.

It wasn't just Leverhulme who wanted to intervene. In 1911 Parliament had authorised the Board of Agriculture for Scotland to acquire some of the Lewis farms and divide them into crofts. In 1917 the Board promised to implement its plans at the end of the war. But the new owner refused to countenance them. He planned a fish-canning plant, new roads and even forestation. The work got underway. Houses were built for workers, harbours were updated, cars, buses and lorries were seen for the first time. Cottonmills and ironworks were promised. The roadwork alone gave employment to hundreds. Not only were fish processing centres set up but 400 retail fish shops were purchased on the mainland – MacFisheries Ltd, a company that many Britons will remember in their High Streets until recently.

Never before had so many been engaged in gainful employment, yet resistance and obstructionism continued. In 1920 fifty ex-servicemen raided two farms, built houses and staked out claims. Warrants were issued but never served. The returned soldiers could have had all the crofts they wanted but they used violence. The Secretary of State supported the landgrabs and let it be understood that if raiders were jailed, he would release them. There was further opposition and other raids until the proprietor halted all operations in May 1920. At 86, Lord Leverhulme, who'd had his instincts for unimpeded personal rule reinforced from Port Sunlight to the Congo, was incandescent. In May 1921 he abandoned Lewis but kept Harris and on his death in 1925 the enterprises there were speedily wound up. He had given Stornoway Castle and its surrounds to his creation, the Stornoway Trust. His lordship had blown over £1.4

Overleaf. *Left:* Ewen squints in the glare. Even when overcast the shell sand was dazzling.
***Right:* Not the lost boys. Ewen and Suk check progress.**

HEBRIDEAN GURKHA

million of his own money vainly trying to shape the Hebrides in his own image. There is, though, a dour, downright stubborn streak throughout the Highlands and Islands which can be so hostile it won't take money if it is seen to be demeaning. Only a wilfully blind outsider would have failed to notice.

The offices at Leverburgh (old name, Obbe, or in Gaelic, An t-Ob) that the Gurkhas were passing today, had once employed some smart Port Sunlight typists who were condemned – poor girls – from the pulpit as 'harlots and concubines of Lever, running about the streets.'

Dhal's pipes could be heard blowing towards us as we neared the finish, and his figure became clear. A group of kids sat on a high bank of lobster creels watching as we tramped in – Central Casting on its toes, obviously. It was less the Relief of Mafeking and more *Ice Cold In Alex*, but it was a triumph in its way. We'd walked the length of the Long Island and could afford to smile. We'd been asked not to look at the camera – though the boys started waving and giving it thumbs up which I thought looked entirely appropriate and the producer, my dears, later agreed. I was interviewed for about two minutes, standing on the slipway, with the sun in the west and its rays bouncing off the water.

Iain never interrupted and allowed me to drone on, making the obvious comments on the Scot-Gurkha mutual respect, and the friendship we'd experienced from every single passing vehicle. 'We're often asked why we have come here, and I always answer, "because of this" and point to the landscape.' I reckoned he would have to edit all this oratory down to about twenty seconds and wondered whether any of it would be good enough.

Of more than passing interest was that Prince Charles had hand-written us a letter of good wishes which made mention of my 'ninety-year-old knees'. How dare the Heir Apparent make such jointist remarks! And him Lord of the Isles too! Of course, we were flabbergasted and thrilled to receive the letter, but when I produced it I thought Suk was going to faint clean away. Prince Charles is highly regarded among Gurkhas and there is every sign that it is far from one-way. Why would HRH write to the likes of me otherwise? We were very grateful and proud to receive the acknowledgement – though one woman wrote to me asking how much he charged for his image to be reproduced in the Gurkha Welfare Trust publications. I wrote back telling her not to be so daft; this was Prince Charles not David Beckham.

None of the boys wanted to be interviewed but I went up to Dhal. 'All you've got to do is say "Thank you Scotland! We're having a wonderful time!" and smile.' This was done in two ticks and with their own thumbs up the Grampian TV boys departed.

Arrival at the hotel was memorable for the stony mountains behind. Lit up by the evening sun they were now bathed in gold and looked as if they were from an utterly different but benign planet. It was a backdrop of other-worldly beauty set in a gin-clear atmosphere that made us wonder just where in the universe we were.

During supper, a young, tweedy stranger came straight up to the table and addressed us in fast Nepali as if in charge. It was the doctor, Dr Christie, who had supplied Ram with the knee support. Kesh, Ram, Suk and Nugendra agreed to the invitation to go round to his house half an hour later but with a blankness that was nearly rude. 'Dhanyabad, Ketaharu!' Thank you, Boys, I hissed before they reacted like forgetful school kids. The whole Christie family spoke fluent Nepali, including the two children. Everyone had a fantastic evening singing Nepalese folk songs – a popular past time of both Nepalese and Hebridean communities. The lads returned wondering how many more coincidences could happen in a week.

Ewen and Dhal disappeared with fishing rods but returned early. The midges were out, and we took time for a wee wander round tiny Tarbert. This was no more than buildings set around a village square with war memorial and quayside but had an interesting history. Both Compton Mackenzie's second and third wives, Chrissie and Lily, came from here, while Borve Lodge, Leverhulme's seat was nearby, as is Amhuinnsuidhe Castle, built in 1886 by the Earl of Dunmore. At the time of our visit it was being sold by the Bulmers Cider heir, along with 50,000 acres, for four million pounds. It was once rented by J. M. Barrie just after the Great War where he wrote a fey drama, *Mary Rose*, the Isle that wanted to be loved, about the nearby Scarp.

It is Scarp that has perhaps the craziest tale attached to it of all the

Western Isles, for it was here that took place the world's first ever inter-island rocket mail experiment. That the glittering attempt to push back the frontiers of technology happened in the Outer Hebrides should warn the reader that the tale did not end in glory. It may be putting it a tad strongly but for a brief moment Scarp was involved in a progress that would culminate in Neil Armstrong's 'giant leap for mankind'.

One July day in 1934 caught Harris unprepared for the arrival of German rocket scientist Gerhard Zucha, along with patron Herr Dombrowsky and hordes of pressmen to witness the vital experiments. The excitement was colossal, so much so that the GPO even sent the postmaster from Lochmaddy to attend the trials. No kidding. This was big stuff. The apparatus was set up on a stretch of sand below the Scarp schoolhouse and the hollow rocket was loaded with letters and parcels. These were no ordinary missives. There were four addressed to King George V, and the Harris Branch of the British Legion sent a message of loyal greetings to the Prince of Wales.

These were all to be fired to the mainland of Harris in the mighty steel rocket. At some point somebody should have asked as to the sense in entrusting formal messages to such a highly untrustworthy, nay untested, means of transport. There was also an envelope addressed to the Secretary of State for Scotland which enclosed two prime herring and a note exhorting him to eat more herring and persuade the rest of the country to do the same. Nobody seemed to spot the inadvisability of even this, despite the fact that no one in their right mind normally posts herring to anyone, never mind the nation's leaders. The madness affected everyone. Other letters were addressed to the Prime Minister and, with hopeful propriety, the Minister of Air.

How come no one spotted the sheer impracticality of rocket mail? Where exactly and how exactly was it going to land? Wouldn't it be better to send mail a less hazardous way? Weren't rockets normally associated with big bangs and destruction? The suspicion is that the locals were having a good laugh and looked forward to either a spectacular success or a wonderful disaster. Either way, it would be a thrilling show that would beat the Mod for entertainment value hands down.

When the great moment came, the inventor retired to a hollow and crouched dramatically over the trigger mechanism. 'The crowd watched closely,' described the *Stornoway Gazette*, 'eager to see the mail shoot forward on its journey. The button was touched, there was a dull explosion and flash of fire. For a second smoke obscured everything but when it cleared the firing apparatus was seen in ruins on the beach: the steel rocket in the midst torn and twisted and the letters strewn about the sand, many of them charred and burnt. Someone in the crowd laughed.' Frankly, I find it hard to credit that only a single person found this funny.

The Hebrides had to wait until the 1960s for a rocket that worked (the heroically-named Corporal missile) but London was less fortunate. As the war clouds gathered, Herr Zucha moved to Peenemunde where his peaceful postal rocket metamorphosed into the lethal V2 under the beady eye of Wernher von Braun. Compton Mackenzie later encapsulated the story in *Rockets Galore!* which, to his irritation, sold more than his serious books. It was made into a film in 1957. Scarp now lies deserted – the last families only left in 1971 – but the schoolhouse still stands, its days in the headlines long gone. When the mighty Saturn V rockets lifted Apollo 11 off the pad at Cape Kennedy in 1969, not many recalled the early days of experimentation on Scarp. Funny that.

It was time to sleep on it.

CHAPTER FOUR

LEVERBURGH TO BENBECULA

The time was 6.50 a.m., the early morning light was sharply bright and the Sound of Harris glittered across to North Uist. Our ferry was a big ro-ro raft affair with a slim bridge high across the centre. It wasn't certain whether there was room for our vehicle on this sailing. Even though I'd booked months ago, we were told that though the team could go as foot passengers, the van would have to wait for the midday sailing. However, we'd learned that this probably wasn't true; block bookings are made by the various authorities to ensure there is always space for their vehicles. If we turned up we'd surely get aboard.

Ewen and I went over to speak to a Caledonian MacBrayne official. Good news. There was plenty of room for our Caravelle. Ewen announced the fact. 'Except for one thing. You, Campbell, have to grant the captain a small favour which involves bending over in the privacy of his cabin.'

Campbell gave an unsteady grin: 'Och, you two, you're right bastards!'

The ferry took a zigzag route to avoid various reefs marked by vertical poles marked in black and white. The sea was a blue you only dream about. Ewen, Nugendra and I sat on a cold starboard area watching a gannet attack. There was a huge shoal of fish out there and the birds' white bodies were lit up by the low sun as their plunging forms smashed through the surface. These brilliant diving flashes acted as a signal to nearby gannets who arrived like patrolling Catalinas which entered a tight climb, stalled and then fell like spears on the fish below. The cacophony of a feeding frenzy as hundreds of birds plummeted from the sky, like the deadly arrows at Agincourt, was mesmerising. While the sight had a certain beauty, it also held a savage greed.

My phone rang. It was Iain from Grampian TV.

'Neil, you know that story you told me about Dhal poaching a salmon?' What if we dress it up a bit, make it clear that Dhal didn't know he was poaching but sell the story to the *Daily Record.* It'll be great publicity and I'll send on the fee.'

'Hmm, not sure. If we could make it clear that it was done without any criminal intent and if our address appears at the bottom, it might be worth it. I'll phone you back.'

The *Record* is read by half of Scotland. The reach would be enormous and the response perhaps phenomenal. Ewen and I discussed it.

'Yeah, okay, Iain. Let's go with it. We really need the address, remember. The story won't help us much otherwise. For a headline, how about "Gurkha Salmon Gaffe"?' Not exactly 'Adolf Hitler Was My Mother, Admits Duchess', but it would do.

I put away the phone feeling partly anxious but fairly certain that this could work to our benefit.

We were nearly across the skerry-scattered Sound. To my surprise we berthed at, not North Uist, but the Isle of Berneray, although at the connecting causeway. Campbell dropped us at its southern end on the soil of North Uist, the most westerly of the Hebrides. We were as close as we were going to get to America. The coast here can have turtles and coconuts all the way from the Carribean washed ashore. In small boxes on my map were marked St Kilda, forty-one miles away, and Rockall at 230 miles out in the Atlantic.

The land was very low, at least 50% lochan while the sea flooded everywhere it could. We hitched up the haversacks and started walking the lonely road through flat green fields that ran down to the shore. Isolated homes were spread across the distant landscape as if a child had laid out his few toy houses as widely as possible.

'This is … ?' asked Suk.

'North Uist!' replied Dhal with happy firmness. Suk nodded to himself as if trying to remember the name.

'Different from … ?' He pointed north.

'Harris!' Kesh and Nugendra said in unison. Well, well, the boys really did know where they were.

As we passed the first of many little red post boxes, stuck on a pole like a promotion for lollipops, a lark rose, twittering in full summer joy. Shelley's *Blythe Spirit* and surely a good omen. This whole area was an ornithologist's dream; dunlin, teal, shoveler and tufted duck, plus water rail, snipe, redshank and twite are here. This, in addition to mallard, mute swan, moorhen and eider. I was keeping my eyes open for the red-breasted merganser and my old nemesis, the corncrake.

'There are lots of different birds here. Look, that's a lapwing!' I pointed. There were also plenty of oystercatchers too, stabbing the grass alongside. 'We have a type of goose called barnacle goose because people long ago believed they grew in sea shells right here!' Dhal took quite a while to translate this as the hill people of Nepal are understandably short on vocabulary concerning small marine encrustations.

It's a smashing story, and it did indeed originate in North Uist when two top Scottish academics visited the Isles. Friends of Erasmus, Hector Boece, first Principal of Aberdeen University, and Alexander Galloway, his Rector, gravely assured the natural historians of the high Renaissance that barnacle geese were generated from mussels in the Uists.

They had lifted up some seaweed 'full of mussil schellis' and discovered there was 'na fishe' in the shell but 'ane perfit schapin foule. First, they shaw thair heid and feit, and last of all they shaw their plumis and wingis; finaly … they fle in the aire as other fowlis dois.' Remarkable. And for those who saw fit to doubt this extraordinary discovery, they were 'rude and ignorant pepil' – so stop sniggering at the back.

'But why did they believe it?' asked Dhal.

'Because nobody knew where they bred. They go off to the Arctic. People accepted what they wanted to believe.'

'Shells are quite like eggs,' put in Nugendra perceptively.

'You say the same word, don't you? Egg shells and seashells?'

asked Dhal.

I could see what was coming. Perhaps the academics were right. 'Shell is just a word for casing. We use it for artillery shells too.' The lesson? We always want to explain the mysteries of life, no matter how extraordinary the explanation.

The team stopped for a break after five miles where the ferry's access road met the Isle's ring road. From here we'd take the clockwise route to Lochmaddy, keeping the broken shoreline on our left. There were lochs to the horizon but whether we were looking at fresh or seawater, islets or ragged peninsulas, we would never know. High fences raised the boys' expectations of spotting deer – a prospect that never fails to galvanise Gurkhas.

'Have some of this,' I handed round a bag of biltong. Another large packet had disappeared when I had thoughtlessly left it lying in my kitchen and Dhal had grilled the lot before I knew anything about it. My surprise was countered by Dhal's inarguable 'You shouldn't have left it out for us. What did you expect?'

'But didn't you find it hard to chew?' I asked to only blank looks; Gurkhas have wonderful teeth.

The new road was built as relief work during the 1846 famine. Any kind of food, never mind biltong, had always been in short supply in the Hebrides. 'There used to be thousands of people who lived here,' said Ewen. The lads looked wide-eyed at the lonely, now heathery landscape.

'Where did they go?' asked Suk, his eyebrows knitted.

'Glasgow, Canada, America … '

North Uist had always had it tough. It had been part of the estates of Clanranald and had been attacked so severely by the Macleods in the early 1600s that the locals were 'forced to eat horse, doggis, cats and other filthie beasts'. By 1814, Bliadhna an Losgaidh, the Year of the Burning, families from North Uist to Barra were dragged to the transports to Canada by constables. An old woman told the Napier Commission years later: 'Oh dear man, the tears come upon my eyes when I think of all we suffered, and of the sorrows, the hardships and the oppression we came through.'

We trudged off towards Lochmaddy. On our right a great crested grebe and at least one chick chugged across a lochan in silent profile, like a pair of 2s, their reflections sharp as pins. I didn't think much about it at the time but I later discovered that this bird has never been seen further north of Fife and never on the west coast at all, never mind the Hebrides. What I'd witnessed was the Slavonian grebe – no, I'd never heard of it either – which has nested in Scotland only since 1908 and should be nesting in Easter Ross. I felt another letter to the *Reader's Digest Book of British Birds* coming on, but after the last row involving corncrake in Forfar (when the editor told me she suspected I was a crank), I decided against it. However, if you have made a similar sighting, don't let me hold you back.

It was beginning to occur to us that the Hebridean perception of distance was nearly as precise as its approach to time. We had passed the entrance sign to Lochmaddy but it took us a mile to reach the first house, which was about half a mile from the next. An old man in the Hebridean uniform of blue coveralls and wellies greeted us from his front lawn.

'How far to Lochmaddy?' asked Dhal.

'This iss Lochmaddy,' he replied genially.

'The town centre?' received a guffaw.

'That's chust at the end of the road, turn left and the harbour iss about two miles on. You're Gurkhas?' he asked, spotting our shirts. It transpired he was a former Merchant Navy man and had encountered Gurkhas on his travels. 'All good old houses on the Isles were built by returned Merchant Navy men,' he commented. 'If you see a stone and cement barn, ye'll know that the money came from over the seas!'

'That's like us. In my homeland the big houses are owned by Gurkhas,' said Dhal delightedly. 'Have you been to Nepal?'

Our old man laughed. 'No, but I've been to Singapore.' He paused, clearing his throat. 'But then I've never been to Skye either.' I explained, to grins, that he meant the nearby isle, not heaven.

'Like us. We have been all over the world but have seen only a little of Nepal.'

Oppostite: Approaching Benbecula. Suk and Kesh with a pointing Ram.

We reached the junction and turned right, not left to the port, and headed southwest on a slightly superior road under an uncomfortably hot sun. Campbell was supposedly parked ahead of us but we couldn't confirm this as there was no connection for our mobiles. Instead we kept thumping along an adjacent path. Eventually he drove up behind us, having fallen asleep at Lochmaddy.

'I just had a cup of tea and then dropped off. It's a really fantastic wee place. You should have seen it!'

'Campbell, why would we have walked an extra two miles?'

'You'll never guess what. There was a cop wearing one of those stab-proof jackets! In Lochmaddy!'

The vision of a potentially darker side to this small port had clearly excited him.

'And don't tell us – traffic lights too?' joked Ewen.

'Lochmaddy means Loch of the Watch Dogs, not police dogs. The watch dogs are the surrounding reefs whose teeth are ready to rip your keel out!' I said.

'Oh, Neil, you're just so smart, aren't you?' replied Ewen.

'Well, there is something of a consensus.'

At this point Nugendra, as if mediating, said that in Nepal Ewen would call me *jetta*, first-born son, whilst adding *dai* to show respect. 'As in, "o jetta dai,"' he explained helpfully, to universal snorts.

As boys, Gurkhas seldom hear their names called. Instead they will be referred to as first or second born son. That's because if a name were called over the hillside, evil spirits or a witch might hear it and thereby have the boy within their power; a captured name is a captured soul.

The route across North Uist to the Atlantic was a featureless, heather-covered moor, houseless and level. The Isle's highest spot is only 230 metres high (Arthur's Seat in Edinburgh is 253 metres) but appeared as a substantial peak when set against the otherwise tabletop surround.

After six miles of this we met the other end of the ring road at a junction that would take us south to Benbecula. A small shop provided us with everything from film to fishing line but it was noticeable how much of the foodstuff was canned or processed.

'Where does all your milk come from?' we asked.

The lady smiled, embarrassed. 'From Aberdeen, and all the bread comes from Glasgow.' Alongside our vehicle on the ferry had been vans stencilled with the likes of Joe's Pies, Glasgow, or Jimmy's Macaroons, Falkirk. It all made sense now. There was still a dearth of fresh food in these parts.

The seven of us sat on a stonewall outside eating ice cream like a row of schoolboys – we were on holiday, after all – as I took the opportunity to phone *The Scotsman*. Joanna Lumley had written us several letters of support. One described our 'wonderful walk' as 'going like the clappers – but even at that speed, the beauty of those Isles will leap up and grab you round the Trossachs.' While most know Joanna as a famous actress, every one of my team knew her Gurkha links.

'Her Dad was 6GR?' asked Dhal, meaning 6th Gurkha Rifles.

'Yeah, Major Jimmy Lumley. There's a famous photo of him with Mad Mike Calvert at the Battle of Mogaung in Burma when he was a Chindit. I'll show it to you when we get back. He served with the VC Saheb, Lalbahadur Pun. She was brought up with the Regiment, in Malaya and Hong Kong.'

'Lal Pun?' repeated Dhal, impressed. All Gurkhas know the story of how each of the 26 Gurkha VCs were won.

'Joanna Lumley? Ah, the drunken lady,' sighed Suk sadly. Obviously, not the entire team, I realised, knew La Lumley's Gurkha background.

'Her grandfather was a colonel in the Indian Political Service who lived in Sikkim and actually visited the Dalai Lama in Lhasa itself in the early 1900s,' I said, in my best bet-you-didn't-know-this voice.

'Sikkim?' queried Dhal,' That means he must have lived at Jeylup Lu, and would have crossed the Himalaya through Gobshi.'

I goggled. 'Just how the hell did you know that?'

'You forget, Neil Saheb,' he replied as if reproving a favourite but foolish pupil. 'Many Gurkha families come from Tibet. And Jeylup Lu was where they had the District HQ.'

Ms Lumley has never forgotten Britain's debt of honour to the

Overleaf. *Left:* Dashain. Gurkha girl in national costume.
***Right:* Dashain. Fun spills over as Captain Bhakta Limbu, front, strives to keep order. RMA Sandhurst 2004.**

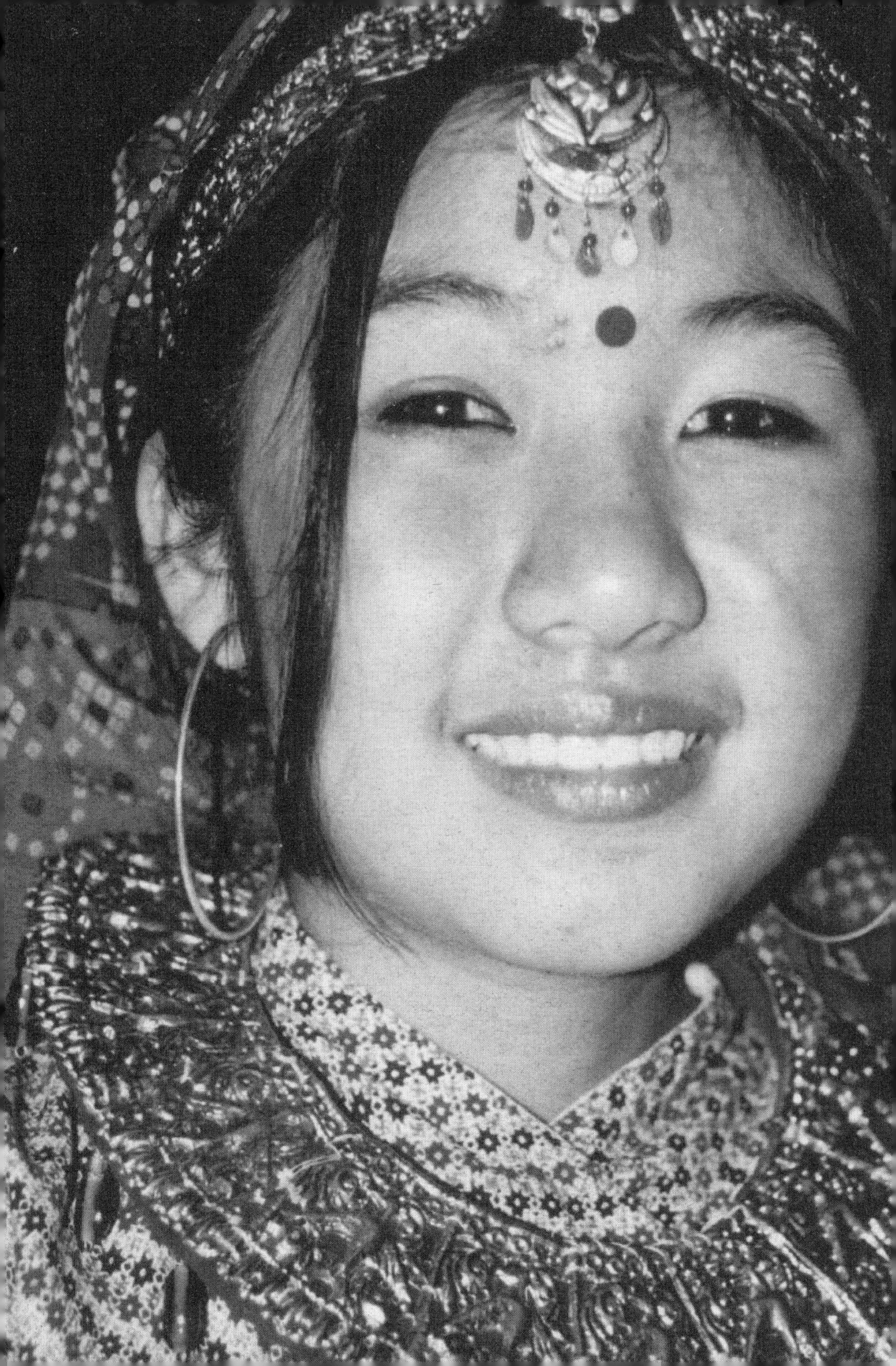

250,000 World War II Gurkhas who served the Crown but were left without a pension. To qualify they would have to have served for fifteen years. Most served only 'for the duration' and received nothing. Other Empire troops were in nearly the same position but payments were made when their countries were made independent. Nepal, however, had never been a colony and, obviously, could not be made independent but its soldiers had served the British Crown and were then left high and dry. Even today they cannot benefit from Commonwealth charities. Our walk was raising funds for the Gurkha Welfare Trust which pays a pension to the surviving 10,500 men and widows. The £5 per week may not seem much but it can be the difference between survival and utter destitution. Plus it means a great deal to these old folk to know that Britain has not forgotten them.

There has not been a single one of our six walks that has not seen cheques and messages of goodwill wing their way from Joanna, who allows even the likes of me to quote her support. Frankly, her name ensures that every press release is read and the subsequent publicity reflects this. This, as you can imagine, electrified Simon Pia at *The Scotsman* and ensured further coverage the following day.

By now it was mid-afternoon and the sun was blazing, but we had about eight miles of foot-slogging to Benbecula. The unavoidable monotony of road walking was broken by our first donors of the day who, in some cases, must have been driving up and down to find us. One lady even brought a family album of her father's time with Gurkhas. Another had small black and white photos of beheaded goats which apparently harked back to Dashain, North West Frontier, 1936.

Nugendra, Suk, Kesh and Ram thought this enchanting. Dhal smiled evilly as if he himself had decapitated the animals.

Dashain is still the biggest celebration in the Nepalese calendar. It compares to Christmas for feasting, singing and gift-giving. Celebrated in honour of Durga, Goddess of Victory and a special figure for Gurkhas, Dashain is observed by all Hindus. The story goes that a monster named Mahishasura was roaming the world and Lord Shiva was obliged to create Durga to destroy it. The goddess had nine pairs of arms and each hand carried a weapon. Mahishashura also possessed superhuman strength and could change into different animals too. After a fight of several days it changed into a buffalo which Durga beheaded with one stroke of her *konras*, sword.

Though it's a national celebration, Gurkhas regard it as a warrior's festival when until recently the soldiers would shave their heads, have their weapons blessed and behead a buffalo at midnight – with a kukri, obviously, and with a single blow for luck. Goats would be next in line. Today there are no decapitations (in the UK at least) but the singing, dancing, drinking and eating still go on until dawn when all men part for the temple to receive a *tika* mark on their forehead.

I've attended two of these extraordinary (no sacrifice) events and found them more family-affirming events than military, where the kids wear their wonderfully colourful national costumes and provide half the entertainment. One mild October evening I found myself in the Gurkha married quarters at Sandhurst where every window was lit up with fairy lights and front doors bore pictures of goddesses. 'This is Durga with, er, friendly snakes,' explained my friend, Omprashad Pun, before we joined hundreds of his colleagues with their families for a fabulous party and concert. The different clans, *jhats*, performed their traditional dances and folk songs and there was even a fairly good pop group. Most acts featured kneeling teenage daughters whose hands performed all those wavy Hindu movements which were unceasingly graceful. When the curtain first jerked open we witnessed small singing children holding lit candles. The intention was that these would be slowly gyrated in front of them, but they got out of sync and began to elbow each other with obvious irritation to the point that it transformed into an unwitting comedy act. The food was wonderful too. As one of only three *goras*, I could appreciate just how different Nepalese culture was, but I also was privileged to be part of it. As a guest of honour, I was presented with a long yellow pure silk scarf which was splendidly colourful but unfortunately not the type of thing a chap can wear down to the pub. The religious side was not overlooked, and though no one shaves his head these days, the men all bore tika marks at breakfast.

At last we approached Benbecula. The route swerved to the left and then right as it hopped across two small isles via three causeways.

Exhaustion was taking its toll, and I was glad to have North Uist behind me but the step of my colleagues seemed as fresh as when we'd stepped ashore that morning. Our arrival had been enlivened by Tornado fighter bombers making simulated runs on RAF Benbecula. Coming in low from the East, they'd hit the afterburners and soar into the sun with a roar that obliterated conversation for miles around.

We crossed the last causeway to where Campbell awaited. It had been built in 1960 while that between Benbecula and South Uist was constructed in 1942 when the airstrip had been laid out – with the proviso that it could take Flying Fortresses. Compton Mackenzie had complained to his friend, Sir Archibald Sinclair, Air Minister, about the 'human offal' and 'phantoms of crime and disease' who were the 'dregs of labour' sent to build the place. In the late 1950s it was a base for rocket testing and later missile firing. The influx of so many mainlanders had given cause for concern but most found the Naafi a godsend. For a start, it had the only chemist south of Stornoway.

'At last, a Gaelic name!' I said. 'Benbecula, mountain of the fords, though that hill over there, Rueval, is Norse.'

'Are we in Catholic country yet?' asked Campbell, a man with his own domestic Rangers' shrine and sensitive to such matters. It would probably trouble his soul to know that on nearby South Uist, on another Rueval, was a thirty foot statue of Our Lady of the Isles, erected in 1957, which brought predictable outcry from the Free Church who regarded it as 'a malign influence on the landscape.'

'This word you keep using, Neil? Norse?' questioned Dhal: 'Is it Norwegian?'

'Old Norwegian, yes. Shouldn't be too surprising, English has lots of Norse. Wednesday, Thursday and Friday are named after Norse gods.'

'Really?' Dhal seemed struck to hear that Europeans had more than one god. 'And what is this Catholic?'

'Ah, now that's a question I'll hand to Campbell!'

Standing round the van, knowing the day's walk was done, had an invigorating effect all of its own. The last of the tea was shared with a lifted bonhomie. The morning's ferry trip seemed so long ago it could have been last week, while last week itself was a blurred memory. The sustained drive and constant attention to hundreds of small details meant that when now became then, their memories were dumped like yesterday's papers.

'Gather round, guys, listen in,' I announced, using a military phrase. To my surprise I was suddenly surrounded by five earnest faces, though Ewen and Campbell folded arms and smirked like two old sweats. 'These are your rooms for tonight. It's not the same as Harris. Ewen and Campbell. Dhal and Ram. Suk, Kesh and Nugendra. While I'm having a room to myself!' Who's smirking now? Little did I know, this was to be a major blunder.

We filled up at a petrol station set amongst the military's family homes which could have been married quarters anywhere: Aldershot, Germany or York, they all have the same slightly shabby air.

'Was this weather forecast?' asked Campbell of the sales girl.

'Nah,' she grunted.

'Nice chat-up line,' grinned Ewen. Campbell sighed at this heartlessness while Dhal snorted to smother the giggles.

Our hotel was nearly at the southern end of South Uist and was a low lying 1960s building whose décor was straight from Crossroads. Still, it would surely do for two nights? The gods punished me for my selfish choice of the single room though. It was the size of a toilet, except it didn't have one, and was downright grubby. I've known less salubrious bus stops. I was furious; a shower or a quick pee would involve an inconvenient walk down the corridor. The other rooms, of course, were magnificent en suite, thickly-carpeted affairs which upset me so much I couldn't bear to go into them. Ewen, Campbell, Suk, Nugendra, Ram, and, I'm afraid, Kesh, thought this about the funniest moment of the day.

After showering, we all sat outside round a little wooden table in the sun, drinking tea. We always wore clean navy blue polo shirts in the evening, with or without our grey Hebridean Gurkha sweat shirts, and tonight was no different. The team liked the blue and grey combination, and was always proud to wear the crossed kukris. The surrounding fields

Overleaf. *Left:* South Uist. Counting late-night sheep might have helped us sleep soundly, but I doubt it.
***Right:* South Uist shore at 10 p.m. Serenity manifest.**

were hedgeless and marked out with posts and wire. As flat as Holland, they could have been polders except they stretched from the Atlantic to a low knobbly range of hills that ran the length of the east coast like the backbone of a giant dragon.

'There's a pool table inside,' confided Suk. Somehow pool has an irresistible hold on our Nepalese colleagues and is one of the few circumstances where peacetime Gurkhas seem ready to intimidate others if they appear ready to compete for a spare table. Given that the midges were already gathering, it seemed a good time to go inside.

The hotel had a large stone-flagged public bar with a couple of the coveted tables – and both unoccupied. The usual cheerful taunts and challenges were made, and the tournament was begun before even the beers had been ordered. There were four beefy drinkers at the bar who eyed Dhal and me with obvious suspicion. 'Am bheil Gaidhlig agaibh?' 'Have you the Gaelic?' asked one so unpleasantly that I was taken aback and cheekily replied in Nepali. This was going to be awkward. His three pals suddenly gasped and pointed to the TV over my shoulder. There in full colour was a close up of me. It was our Grampian TV piece right on cue!

'Ketaharu, yaha chito!' 'Guys, here quick!'

There was a scramble of Gurkhas. We watched entranced as our images told the story of our trek. It must have lasted for four minutes. I appeared surprisingly relaxed and the cameraman, by use of judicial close ups, had made the kids at Leverburgh resemble a happy throng. The team was unexpectedly tiny set against the sweeping Harris horizons but Dhal looked particularly cool on the pipes and his happy 'Thank you Scotland! We're having a wonderful time!' ended the piece on a cheery high. This was the type of introduction that a man should have every time he goes into a strange bar. Our fellow drinkers were more than impressed. They sat there, open-mouthed, as if we'd just pulled the best con trick of all time. Either that or were we genuine TV stars. And we could play the pipes too! 'Jay-sus, suas am piobaire!' Up the piper 'Slàinte mhath!' 'Slàinte mhòr!'

Supper was not very clever. The fare was plain, freezer to micro stuff, and the only hit was a starter of crab claws in ginger. We asked for these for the following night and were glad we did; they had none left but would specially order for us. All these Isles were surrounded by the best seafood in the world. This was the country in microwave microcosm. It didn't have to be. Harris had shown us that.

When we put away our napkins (and Ram had gathered up the khursani) the group headed back to the bar to find it full of people drinking whisky, mostly with bagpipes, as this was a convention of Scottish stereotypes. Bagpipes? What was going on? As we edged through the crowds, I bumped into a piper I know from Edinburgh. Now, this was getting seriously weird. He was speaking Gaelic – a language I didn't even know he possessed. Being somewhat fu' (well, I knew he was fond of the cratur), he took a few moments to recognise me but explained that there was a musical gathering in three days time in Barra and that this was some sort of prequel. Pipers began to play in various corners of the room which added considerably to the sense of bedlam. A wonderful, fantastic bedlam though, which isn't encountered in any of the tourist ceilidh theme bars. Dhal, Ram and I took our drinks to a table near the door where a serious-looking couple aged about eighteen were sitting, a set of Northumbrian pipes between the guy's knees.

Dhal and Ram were like excited terriers, pipers surrounded by pipers, and gave the young couple curious looks.

'Hi,' I said, 'Could you show your pipes to my friends from Nepal?'

The couple looked uneasy and I suddenly realised they were nervous of Dhal and Ram. We'd never encountered this before and part of me wanted to laugh. They were from the north of England and probably on their first ever holiday together.

Dhal's grin can appear surprisingly evil, I thought, and they practically flinched when he smiled and requested, 'Could you play them, please?'

'My friends are both pipers but have never seen these before,' I added, as if this would make things easier. It did. Within moments the lad was playing away. Minutes later Dhal and Ram rushed off to grab their own pipes and were soon merrily blasting the roof off and making dozens of friends in the process. Affixed with solid silver and at least a hundred years old, their instruments were sources of awe – and both guys were in that superstar category of working pipers. Dhal had played at the Queen

Mum's hundredth birthday at Horse Guards and was a qualified tutor while Ram had twenty years of regimental piping behind him. They might have played for fun but they didn't only play for fun – and it showed. These pipers two, our secret or not so secret PR weapon, were a hell of an entrance ticket to local society.

An evening's drinking though wasn't on my agenda, and as the sun was still shining, I decided to take a stroll to see the nearby beach which I knew to be one of those enormous white ones which would be magnificent at this time of the day. The unsurfaced track began in a haze of gold, the houses few and while a couple of people nodded in greeting, there was something wrong. The dunes didn't seem to be getting any closer. I hadn't brought a map and had merely trusted my judgement. The low horizon had fooled me; it was over two miles across rabbit-run greensward until I reached the shore, but my ramble was wonderfully vindicated. I sat on the fine white sand, taking in the ozone-rich air with the sun still hanging above a sighing Atlantic in a gentle blaze of silvers and reds. Small clouds were lit up like temple burners. The shore ran a hundred yards to the sea and disappeared on both sides like a cream runway. I was totally alone. Serenity held my head in its hands and a wave of bliss washed over me. This was the effect of the Outer Hebrides at 10 p.m. Was there anyone on the planet as blessed as me?

Back at the hotel the bar was still going like a fair. Dhal could be seen from the window blowing away. Can life improve? We were going to find out.

CHAPTER FIVE

BENBECULA TO ERISKAY

It was no surprise to find that breakfast at our Crossroads Motel was heavy on baked beans. 'I know a major in the Argylls that once asked the officers' mess steward for beans at breakfast only for the steward to tell him, in a horrified voice, that this would be impossible, "'cos baked beans is not a hofficer's vegetable,"' I said.

We all laughed but Suk, slightly puzzled, asked, 'So Sahebs don't eat beans?'

'It's a class thing,' explained Ewen, 'Like having your tea, supper or dinner. Even Americans don't understand it.'

'Beans are for us lower orders,' added Campbell.

'Speak for yourself!' snapped Ewen.

'What is dog's bollocks?' asked Suk out of the blue. We tried to frown. 'Is the same as dog's breakfast?'

'No, it isn't. And don't ever muddle the two.'

Forsaking the road for the day, we headed for the huge Atlantic beaches. South Uist is obviously Catholic. As soon as we crossed the causeway the first thing we passed was a shrine with Mary and the Christ

Overleaf. *Left:* Suk approaches fishing buoy having learnt not to give it a flying kick.
***Right:* Dhal contemplates another soaking.**

HEBRIDEAN GURKHA

Child. The boys always like to pay due reverence to any religious objects and it crossed my mind that they were going to give it the usual hands-together prayer greeting that would look extremely odd to any passer by. They didn't, but clearly approved of what they perceived to be a wayside god and goddess.

Clouds hovered high over the sea and occasional formations of oystercatchers, art deco on the wing, scorched past bleating in excitement. Waves threw themselves on the sand in immense slow-motion yawns as we skipped past. We were totally alone. The map warned that this was a missile test area but there were no warning flags and the observation huts were bleakly empty. The boys sang folk songs with one taking the lead and the others acting as chorus. Most entailed lonely hillboys and their sweethearts. The favourite seemed to repeat the words jam-jam-jama-jam that I knew. Jam means blink but in this song – ah, you're ahead of me – refers to the fluttering eyes of a beautiful girl.

Our football was carelessly kicked far ahead again and again. I was reminded of the incongruity between these gentle, romantic and social lads and their bloodthirsty place in military history. I had come across the following in an old book: 'The Gurkhas are courageous and even reckless … faithful small combatants, (with their) formidable national arm called a khoukri. Though they fight with ferocity… the Gurkhas know how to be generous and courteous.' That this comes from the *Empire Book for Boys 1917*, from a time of unthinking racism when praise was almost never given to foreigners, but accurately describes the Gurkhas' main characteristics, tells me a lot about the long-standing regard we have for these wee men. Almost the entire British nation has never met one. Few people or publications promote them, yet their standing is so high that you only have to mention the name for people to smile or nod knowingly. On my various treks, both men and women have shaken hands with my Gurkha pals and declared it an honour – and really meant it. Who else fits this category of affection, or even comes close? Answer? No one. They are a special breed. We're lucky to have them and Ewen, Campbell and I must be luckier than most to count some as close friends.

'No, Suk! Don't kick it!' I yelled, waking from my reverie by the sight of Suk about to take a flying kick at a fishing buoy. He stopped in mid flight, eyes wide and white against his brown skin, as he turned to check with me. 'That's solid! Pick it up and see!' I shouted.

Suk lifted it up, rather over-did the mime of realising it was unexpectedly heavy but then rolled it like he was in a bowling alley complete with all the arm actions and flighty pose. The shore, with the tide way out, was a perfect surface and the buoy rolled in a straight line at a steady speed for fifty or so yards. I have no idea where they got them from, but suddenly Nugendra had two more and we were in the middle of a bowls tournament. We were laughing like hyper-active kids for a full ten minutes before moving on. I'd known these guys for less than a week, but the singing and high spirits reminded me that we seemed like old friends. We'd keep in touch for years to come.

A rain storm appeared out of nowhere and drenched us all but no one seemed to notice. The sun came and went and there were always blue patches tantalisingly blowing through the sky. The sensation of space was practically hallucinogenic but the abiding effect was the air; it was airy like we'd never been outdoors before. It swamped our lungs so that every artery pumped with an oxygen-rich rush that quickened the step and lifted the heart. When the sun came out it flushed us with a dazzling light and transformed the sea to a South Pacific turquoise. The enormous heaven above was from a giant's catalogue and the sense of being on the edge of the map, Europe, and even the world, was hard to fight.

A rare headland compelled us to leave the shore. 'Let's cut across here to the next beach?' suggested Dhal, and within minutes we found ourselves in sunny, unfenced, flower-filled meadows, straight from a dream. The heady sweetness of golden clover – not red or white, but gold – hit us like a wall of honey. The scent drifts way out to sea where landfall is flagged in the most pleasant way possible, perhaps. The boys threw themselves down like puppies, laughing, and rolled about as if overcome by euphoria.

Ram pointed at some rabbit burrows: 'For haggis?'

'Oh yes,' Ewen said, and the others instantly, unspoken, understood

Overleaf. *Left:* Machair madness. the wish to roll in the flowers was exuberantly unstoppable.
***Right:* Horizons of Heaven. Moved but still on the move.**

what was going on. 'They're quite common round here. Keep your eyes open.'

Ram nodded seriously. If there were any haggis off guard today, he'd be the very man to bag them. To my knowledge, no live haggis has ever escaped the clutches of an alert Gurkha. Honest.

When we all leapt over a burn, it seemed the longest jump of our lives, slower than the normal speed, and when each of us finally hit the bank of flowers, the crash landing came with an explosion of laughter. Had we regressed to being six years old or were we high on some Hebridean elixir?

When we encountered the stone skeleton of an old cottage, we quickly understood just how much history South Uist encompassed, for this was Gearraidh Bhailteas, the birthplace of Floraidh, or Flora, MacDonald in 1722.

Flora was descended from the chiefs of Clanranald, schooled in Edinburgh, mixed with polite society and was well versed in the politics of the day. When Bonnie Prince Charlie came knocking in 1746 after the catastrophe of Culloden, because her father was in Government service Flora was allowed a permit to cross the Minch to Skye. They set sail on 28 June from North Uist on the journey that was to inspire *The Skye Boat Song* with its lyrics 'over the sea to Skye – though many erroneously believe, being mainlanders, that any trip to Skye could only have come from the mainland.

Just a few miles away from where we stood the Prince had slept on the heather, experiencing hunger and scurvy which brought on bleeding gums and ulcerated legs and was tormented by midges. Clanranald provided fresh clothing, provisions and rifles. The Prince spent the days watching the warships in the Minch looking for him (one day he counted fifteen), fishing or shooting grouse. He also got through a bottle of brandy a day.

Famously, Charlie was in female dress on the trip to Skye, disguised as Flora's maid, Betty Burke. When they arrived at Kingsburgh on Skye, the lady of the house was taken aback at 'her' appearance and asked, 'What a long odd lassie was this?' Flora and the Prince parted at Portree, 1 July, with him declaring: 'Madam, we shall meet at St James's yet,' referring to St James's Palace, London. They never, in fact, met again.

Flora was soon arrested and after her release from the Tower of London married Kingsburgh's son, Allan, by whom she bore at least nine children. In 1773 Flora's most famous, if improbable, guests were Dr Johnson and Boswell. The latter described her as 'a little woman of genteel appearance and uncommonly mild and well bred.' While Dr Johnson (who delighted in the 'Tochter Shonson' address) saw her as 'a woman of middle stature, soft features, gentle manners and elegant presence.' The good doctor slept in the same room and bed as that on which Charlie had lain on his flight twenty-seven years earlier.

The next year Allan and Flora emigrated to the Carolinas where, ironically, Allan fought for the Hanoverians in the War of Independence and was even taken prisoner. In 1779 they returned to Kingsburgh. Flora died in 1790, aged 68. In her will she asked to be buried in the linen sheet in which the prince had slept. This was done and thousands came to her funeral at Kilmuir, not far from where she and 'Betty' had landed on Skye. On her tombstone is carved the tribute that that high Tory, Dr Johnson, had paid her: Flora MacDonald, Preserver of Prince Charles Edward Stuart. Her Name Will Be Mentioned in History And if Courage and Fidelity Be Virtues, Mentioned With Honour.

We were a strange tribute group. The story of bravely hoodwinking the authorities was received with approval, but the memorial tablet explained – and overlooked more important facts – that at Flora's death the mourners here in South Uist took only a week to drink 300 gallons of whisky! Way to go! The lads were most impressed.

'This land, Neil, is very good. Why don't people farm here properly?' asked Dhal almost confidentially, surveying the low green land as if considering its purchase.

'The soil is rubbish here, too thin,' I began, 'And the Outer Hebrides is too far away from everything. Notice how everyone we meet is a pensioner? The young simply go. Farming is too hard work for too little money.' In fact, in the Western Isles 26.6% are aged over 60 – the highest

Overleaf. *Left:* Flora MacDonald's birthplace. Campbell joins us to inspect the ruin.
Right: **Shore thing. Oystercatchers seemed as excited as we were.**

percentage in the UK. Of the scattered houses, over 17% are single pensioner households and 7% are holiday homes.

'But you said that once 55,000 lived here. Now only 26,000? In my country our numbers grow but we don't leave the land,' he waved at the empty landscape.

'Yeah, but here we have much higher expectations in life and we have the opportunity to escape. There are 5,000 crofts in these Isles, that's nearly 80% of the land but over 90% of them provide less than two days' work a week. The average size is tiny: seven and a half acres. You can't live on that!'

The end of the Clan Ranald era in the Uists began in 1794 when the chief, Reginald George MacDonald, succeeded as a minor, from a father who was to be the last to live among his clan. The estates paid him an annual rent of £25,000 and had been in the family for five centuries, but by 1827, after thirty years of London high living, and representing an English rotten borough, he found himself on the verge of bankruptcy.

In 1837 South Uist was sold to Lt Colonel John Gordon of Cluny Castle in Aberdeenshire for £84,000. Barra was sold to the same man in 1838 and Benbecula in 1839. Cluny cleared tenants off his land but matters came to a head in the 1840s' potato blight. A Government investigator reported on the Gordon estates and found scenes of horror. 'An awful reflection – that at this moment a wealthy inheritor of this island is not employing poor people,' and predicted that 'scenes will occur in SUist, Barra and Benbecula which would be disgraceful to his name, and injurious to the reputation of Great Britain.'

Gordon was written to by a Government official who threatened 'to interpose in favour of the sufferers ... leaving Parliament to decide whether or not you should be legally responsible for the pecuniary consequences of this just and necessary intervention.' The Colonel reacted only by employing men on his estates in return for meal, but the 1847 potato famine led to him forcibly shipping upwards of 2,000 persons from South Uist and Barra to Quebec and turned adrift between 1848-51. Other destitutes trudged to Inverness to find safety of sorts in the Poor House.

Colonel Gordon bequeathed the 100,000 acres to his son, John Gordon, but he died young and his wife inherited the estate, remarried a

Sir Reginald Cathcart and became known as Lady Gordon Cathcart. She set out to prove her former father-in-law was a pussy cat. Persuaded to give land in South Uist to build a hospital, she reluctantly gave a quagmire but with the spiteful condition that it be built between 1st November and 31st January. Her scheme was thwarted by heavy frost which meant carts could transport the necessary stone, and the building was completed. The money came from the Marquess of Bute and was staffed by nuns.

Lady Gordon Cathcart visited her properties just once in fifty-four years but this did not prevent her from ensuring that ten land raiders on Vatersay were jailed. Unbelievably, she survived until 1935.

Nowadays most of the land is subject to crofting tenure and the big estate owners have very little land all to themselves, though they have shooting and fishing rights, plus quarries.

None of this seemed to surprise my Gurkhas. Probably because bonded labour only ended in Nepal in 2000 there was a cultural assumption that large landowners were only cruel. That our two nations had a shared background of deprivation was of little joy.

Fatalism is an outlook common to both Nepal and Gaeldom. Events, both sides believe, are predestined. In Gaelic it is Freasdal, Providence, while in Nepali it is Bhagya, Fate. As Gaels respond to life's set backs with 'Bhae an Dain!' 'It was predestined!' Gurkhas exclaim: 'Yatina samma pugna bhanero lekheko ranecha.' 'It must have been written down that I go so far and no further.'

We had spent longer than expected at Flora MacDonald's birthplace, partly because the boys were waking up to the fact that Scotland had a clan-based history with which they identified. Gurkhas come from only 10% of Nepal's population and have an equally strong clan base. The Gurungs, Tamangs, Magars, Rais and other tribes all have singular identities stretching back a thousand years. Though these days tradition is changing, as in the UK, I well remember a corporal proudly telling me that he was descended on both sides from Limbus for ten generations back. Yet still the blood is strong.

Overleaf. ***Left:*** **The sandmen. Suk leads Kesh and Nugendra.**
Right: **In clover. Suk and Nugendra counting daisies or buttercups.**

It was revealing how men of septs of the Limbu clan, such as the Yonghang or the Jabegu, were unthinkingly referred to as Limbus. The clan family tree is better understood by Gurkhas; try asking any Scot to name some septs of Clan Chattan.

The Highland clans were much more complex than is generally portrayed. They changed and modified over time. Patronymics, for instance, only started to be adopted during the thirteenth century when the descendants of Donald, grandson of Somerled, started calling themselves MacDonald. For centuries it was only the blood descendants of the Lords of the Isles who bore the name. The greatest of their war chiefs was only ever known to his Gaelic contemporaries as Alasdair MacColla, after his father Coll MacGillespie. Surnames were largely unknown among the common people until the early eighteenth century when clanship was already in decline. Many adopted the surname of the chief, implying a kinship that had never existed.

Supported by a cattle economy and inspired by a thousand years of legend, the patriarchal society was both benevolent and tyrannous. The chief was the father of the clan, with terrible powers. While there might not have been a better alternative to his protection, there was no appeal against his authority.

Ownership of the land was disputed by hereditary feuds and the chief drew his pride and importance from the number of loyal clansmen who would follow him into battle. The evidence shows that many were proud to be called and to die gloriously if necessary.

Military service was payment in kind for tenants but an Act of 1747 abolished the 'Heritable Jurisdictions' of the chiefs – though guaranteed by the Act of Union. Large numbers of warriors who owed allegiance elsewhere represented a significant threat to central government. General Wade had reported in 1724 that the Highlanders were of questionable loyalty and practised in the use of arms. He was dead right too.

Consequently, clansmen were now obliged to pay rent. They were no longer counted in broadswords but were valued in shillings and pence. It wasn't just the Cheviot sheep but a whole new world of agriculture ready to be ushered in that spelled the end. The new farmers could triple the landowners's rent.

In 1799 Lord MacDonald of Sleat correctly observed that his North Uist estates were uneconomic and created new larger farms which were let to incomers capable of raising bigger harvests and healthier livestock – and thus pay larger rents. The emigration of his better-off, long-established tenants was immediate, despite his complaints of disloyalty. In fact, the departures were to his advantage as a vestigial pauper population was, under Poor Law liability, the responsibility of incoming tenants who would make the removal a precondition of contract.

The near bankrupt Reginald George MacDonald of Clanranald was warned it might be unsafe for him to sell South Uist and Benbecula. He had already removed 800 people from seven townships and 'his' people hated him. As a territorial kin-based society Clanranald had ceased to exist in all but memory. A new clansman had emerged: near starving and useful only as a source of income.

These tales of woe were listened to with sympathy and interest; paradoxically, Gurkhas could empathise more closely than most modern Scots. Nepal's rural backwardness may be attractive to tourists but it is still unbearably medieval. Even now 90% of its population lives off the land with the majority existing at subsistence level.

We'd walked twenty miles over the finest beaches that the Ocean has ever created, and across magical machairs like the plains of heaven, but hadn't come across a single soul. There was not a scrap of litter (bar the fishing buoys) and the air was almost dizzyingly pure under a sky that seemed surreally high. The coastal road lay a couple of miles inland, set behind the usual lochans, but apart from the occasional house the only human evidence had been some ruins and two standing stones. It was as if this enormous length of sand was just ours and the beauty solely for us. How could we be anything other than uplifted to the point of exuberance? No one, not even me, was remotely tired.

With our walking finished, we made a short visit to Eriskay by van, crossing the new causeway opened only months before by Prince Andrew.

Overleaf. *Left:* Looking east. A passing rain storm dramatically back-lights South Uist machair.
***Right:* Edge of the world. Ewen wondering how quickly the tide comes in.**

The Isle is sited like a coccyx at the base of the Uists' spine and is home to a community centre where we found welcome mugs of tea. The late afternoon sun shone on a sparkling sea outside but it was faintly depressing that the other patrons were teenage mothers whose infants were struggling, unattended, with sausage and beans. This whole area should be a spectacularly healthy place in which to grow up.

'See that?' pointed Ewen at a large black and white print of a freighter. 'That's the *SS Politician*. It was wrecked just a few miles away during the war and was full of whisky!'

'Wow! What happened?' asked Dhal, his eyes lighting up at the thought.

It was a prospect that had similarly lit up the islanders back in 1941. The ship had run aground on Calvay, a small isle at the eastern end of the Sound of Eriskay with 24,000 cases of whisky bound for the USA. A massive impromptu salvage attempt was made by the locals and much was brought ashore before the vessel broke up. The story was famously retold by Compton Mackenzie's *Whisky Galore!* but, less famously, some were jailed by the sheriff at Lochmaddy for offences against the excise laws and were sentenced to two months.

'They reckon that the whisky keeps turning up to this day. Not long ago there was an auction of a whole load of bottles,' said Campbell.

'Fantastic!' exclaimed Suk: 'A whole ship of whisky?'

'Yeah, remember this was during the war when there was hardly any of the stuff.'

Even less well known is that the *SS Politician* was carrying 290,000 Jamaican ten shilling notes – the equivalent of several million pounds today. The Crown Agents were confident that none of these would ever get into circulation. Two months later they were turning up in Liverpool. By 1958, the Public Record Office official files say, they had been presented in banks in England, Scotland, Switzerland, Malta, Canada, the US and, of course, Jamaica.

We had only visited Eriskay to say we'd been there but as we drove back everyone craned to see where the ship had been wrecked. I had known the tale for as long as I remember but for the Gurkhas it was yet further confirmation that the Hebrides were a source of stories and legends.

Back at the hotel the bar was as mobbed as if they were giving away the *Politician's* cargo and the pipes were still shattering the smoke-laden atmosphere with a near paralysingly loud series of reels and strathspeys. It was an obliterating sonic tartan. One sensed that this was not going to be a quiet evening, or an early one.

'Yours have a very special tone,' commented one drinker of Dhal and Ram's pipes. 'Age always makes things better,' he added, tapping his whisky glass knowledgeably. The mix of welcoming company and drink with the happy bonus of pipers was an unbeatable combination to all of us.

Suk and Kesh were chatting to two attractive girls and it looked as if Nugendra was ready to start dancing. To Gurkhas, dance is an absolutely fundamental part of any social gathering and they are completely uninhibited about it. Everyone knew who we were, and Dhal was universally referred to as 'the sarchant'.

'Och, he's a fine gentleman, right enough,' said one old man to me, his sweet Gaelic accent adding affection to the words. 'None of ye have been to the Tìr nan Òg afore?' He gave a grave shake of his impressive head. 'Am bheil Gaidhlig agaibh?'

'No, 'fraid not,' I answered: 'I find Nepali difficult enough.'

'A bhalaich' 'O boy', he agreed. In that moment I realised there was a linguistic link between the Language of Eden and that of the Himalaya; they both precede, almost poetically, the vocative 'O' before nouns in greeting or for emphasis. While Gaels say 'A nighinn', 'O daughter', 'A bhalaich', 'O boy', or 'A Mhaighstir', 'A Master', Nepalese use 'O didi', 'O sister', 'O bhai', 'O boy' – or even 'O jetta dai', 'O First Born Son'.

'We've just been to Eriskay for a quick visit, saw where the *Politician* sank,' I explained.

'Chust so?' his eyebrows raised, 'And ye'll be off to Barra the morn? Ye'll soon think the *Politician* grounded there. The fil-lum should neffer been made in Barra.'

I tutted in sympathy; obviously this was a touchy subject. 'Gu leoir',

Overleaf. *Left:* Deserted at Dalabrog. Evening sun lights the scene.
***Right:* Ewen takes shelter from sudden cloud burst.**

HEBRIDEAN GURKHA

'galore', is one of a number of Gaelic phrases which have passed into English but perhaps the ship's story should be avoided round here in any language.

By now the drinkers weren't so much dancing as bouncing into each other as young and old swayed and clapped. Perversely, not a drop of drink was spilled but the party spirit was bubbling over. When the whole hooting assembly arrived in Barra the following night, we were assured, then we'd really see some fun. Apparently there would be the lure of fiddlers too. We wondered quite what state everyone would be in, and on the advisability of a two-day binge prior to the main event. How, too, can whisky play such an important role in social activities when the Outer Hebrides didn't have a single distillery? It seemed a cultural impossibility.

Many hours later I was awoken by the sounds of someone moving about in the dark on the flat roof outside my window. 'Who's there?' I shouted angrily. The footsteps stopped but a voice came: 'I'm locked out. Can you open the front door for me?' Within a minute I was admitting a seriously drunk stranger into the hotel without even knowing whether he was a guest, nor knowing how exactly he had got on to the roof and then down again quite so quickly without hurting himself. Perhaps he flew. Anything seemed possible on these Isles.

CHAPTER SIX

BARRA

The van drove slowly down the main street of Lochboisdale. It was a cloudless morning, before seven, and the couple of miles to the tiny port were lit by the low sun as if today the Divine Lighting Director was in personal charge.

'Look at her!' exclaimed Kesh. We were horrified to see a young woman, apparently unconscious, on her back, half in and half out of a phone box, with one breast exposed.

'Drugs?' wondered Ewen. It was an ugly reminder that not everyone was in our happy loop and that even out here there was a drug problem.

'Do you want me to stop?' asked a concerned Campbell.

There was a pause. 'There's people walking up and down,' I said guiltily.

'They will look after her?' pleaded Suk. There was a horrible silence as we continued to the quayside.

'They can't miss her,' I added flatly, trying to sound soothing. The boys' eyes looked back and forth. There was part of the West that was incomprehensible to Gurkhas. Once a corporal told me, mystified, that he had noticed our beggars all seemed perfectly healthy.

Our ferry was a big, magnificent and near empty beast. Apparently it was the ship that would take us to Oban tomorrow night and we marvelled at the space.

'Look at all this!' waved Nugendra. There were cushion-covered benches, big airplane-type seats, bars, shops and a cafeteria.

'We should sleep all the way,' said Ewen. Thoroughly chuffed by the prospect of a comfortable, nay luxurious, journey home, we congratulated ourselves on our luck. Two days left on the Isles and a proper cruise to round it off. Everyone went on deck to enjoy the sun and watch the low grey stone of South Uist slip away, feeling that our ship had not only come in, it was leaving with us on it for places new too.

Not having anything to do for an hour and a half, we went below to test drive the armchairs. 'Look at these,' pointed Ewen to a glass display case, 'Jimmy Choo shoes in pink Harris Tweed. I expect all the girls in Barra will be wearing them.'

Arrival saw us wake and stir like a heap of healthy dolls that had been thrown on airplane seats. It was 9 a.m. and time to disembark. Castlebay is a row of tiny light and dark houses set like piano keys around the harbour, whose bay holds a handful of small boats and yachts. In the centre is the island stronghold, Kisimul Castle, familiar from *Whisky Galore!* and looked as immovable as ever. On the small hill behind stood Our Lady, Star of the Sea, Catholic church. The weather was perfect; a blue sky and not a breath of wind. No wonder it looked like a film set. It was a film set!

'Postcard time, boys,' I said, as Campbell parked on the seafront, and we trooped into a minute general store which was delightfully heavy on one pound notes and where everything seemed to come in brown paper bags via large glass jars behind the counter. The *Stornoway Gazette* had our picture on the front page, taken at the British Legion on our first night. We looked a shambles and, comically, Dhal's quotes made him sound like Dr Livingstone visiting the benighted natives of Outer Britain. Everyone in the shop knew who we were and it didn't matter that we were only spending a couple of quid.

'I heard you on Radio Scotland this morning. Poaching salmon, eh?' smiled the lady on the till. My pulse suddenly kicked like I'd injected pure adrenalin.

'What?'

'Oh, aye, fly boys youse!'

Opposite. The leaving of South Uist. Our ship had come in.

'But what did they say?' I begged.

'Chust that you'd poached some salmon and it wass all a laugh, I remember the man laughing.'

'When does the *Daily Record* get in?' I exhaled.

'Midday.'

'A bhalaich!'

On the wall outside was affixed a Scottish Film Council metal plaque, commemorating the 1996 centenary of cinema and announcing that Alexander 'Sandy' Mackendrick had made *Whisky Galore!* here. Alongside was a postbox into which I thrust my postcards. To my utter amazement, one arrived at my sister's house in Hampshire the next morning. The van roared up the hill to find our hotel on the far side. Very roughly speaking, Barra is six miles by six, with Castlebay set on the south and our hotel on the north west. Its map would have inspired Robert Louis Stevenson; sand-ringed and set amid a sapphire sea, it was to define the Outer Hebrides for us.

Campbell went the wrong way round the ring road, meaning that it took us twenty instead of ten minutes to arrive at the hotel. The glorious morning and fabulous blonde beaches, dipping into a clear, then exotically blue sea, brought back memories of childhood summers, long ago in an unknown past. It was so entrancingly beautiful that it could not be the present day. I'd slipped back in time; it was already imbued with nostalgia. Only the past can be this perfect.

And there was something old fashioned about the men that were mowing their lawns with manual machines, the boys with those scalped wartime haircuts, Fair Isle jerseys and scuffed knees while strangers smiled and the sun shone as in home movies against an utterly unspoiled landscape. It was as if we'd tapped into a folk memory, the lost ideal from a generation ago. But we were no Lost Boys.

The Isle of Barra Hotel was set against the white sweep of the shell-sand Tangasdale Beach, where it considered the dreamy blue horizon as if auditioning for the title of the world's most glorious hotel location. 'This can't be Britain,' I thought. There had been many moments when I had felt abroad, where the locals only were a bit like us, but this morning was as if we'd unknowingly sailed to a forgotten place lost in time. The island at the bottom of the islands.

Built in 1977 with Highlands & Islands Development Board money, the 40-bedroom hotel was disappointingly ordinary inside, with high white-washed walls hung with tartan rugs.

'This is like Aviemore,' muttered Ewen. He was right. Our rooms were no more than comfortable but depressingly short on character. No matter, the staff was pleasant, the window from our room framed a fabulous view and we were completely happy.

The next stop was the famous Tràigh Mhòr airstrip, a massive expanse of glittering white beach in the north of the Isle which acts as a runway and where aircraft are bound by tide tables. We drove up and parked in the airport's little car park and wandered into the equally petit terminal. Strangely, it bore that universal airport smell. The next flight wasn't for a couple of hours.

The group took to the shore and immediately spotted an abandoned private aircraft, a Piper Cherokee, skulking at the edge of the beach, its wings roped down with sandbags.

'C'mon, let's start it up!' said Dhal, and climbed in with Ram, to take the two front seats. They both pulled on the safety belts as if they'd done this before.

'Okay, Suk, turn the propeller!'

Suk yanked the prop clockwise and it stuttered on its circuit. There was no contact. The only roars were to be, not those of an engine firing, but our laughter. Of course, the occasion required at least a hundred photos with Ram and Dhal posing as debonair pilots, aviator glasses cool, and Suk heroically handling the propeller. The prospect of the Gurkha Air Force was just a contact away.

The football was booted about for a moment, but the heat was just too sapping, the sand too blinding, and a small penalty shoot out was organised: as ever, Scotland v Nepal. There is considerable debate concerning the continued removal of the shell-sand here for building material or chicken feed, as it will in time compromise the airstrip's

Overleaf. *Left:* Castlebay Main Street. Of course it looks like a film set; it is a film set.
***Right:* A plaque marks the spot.**

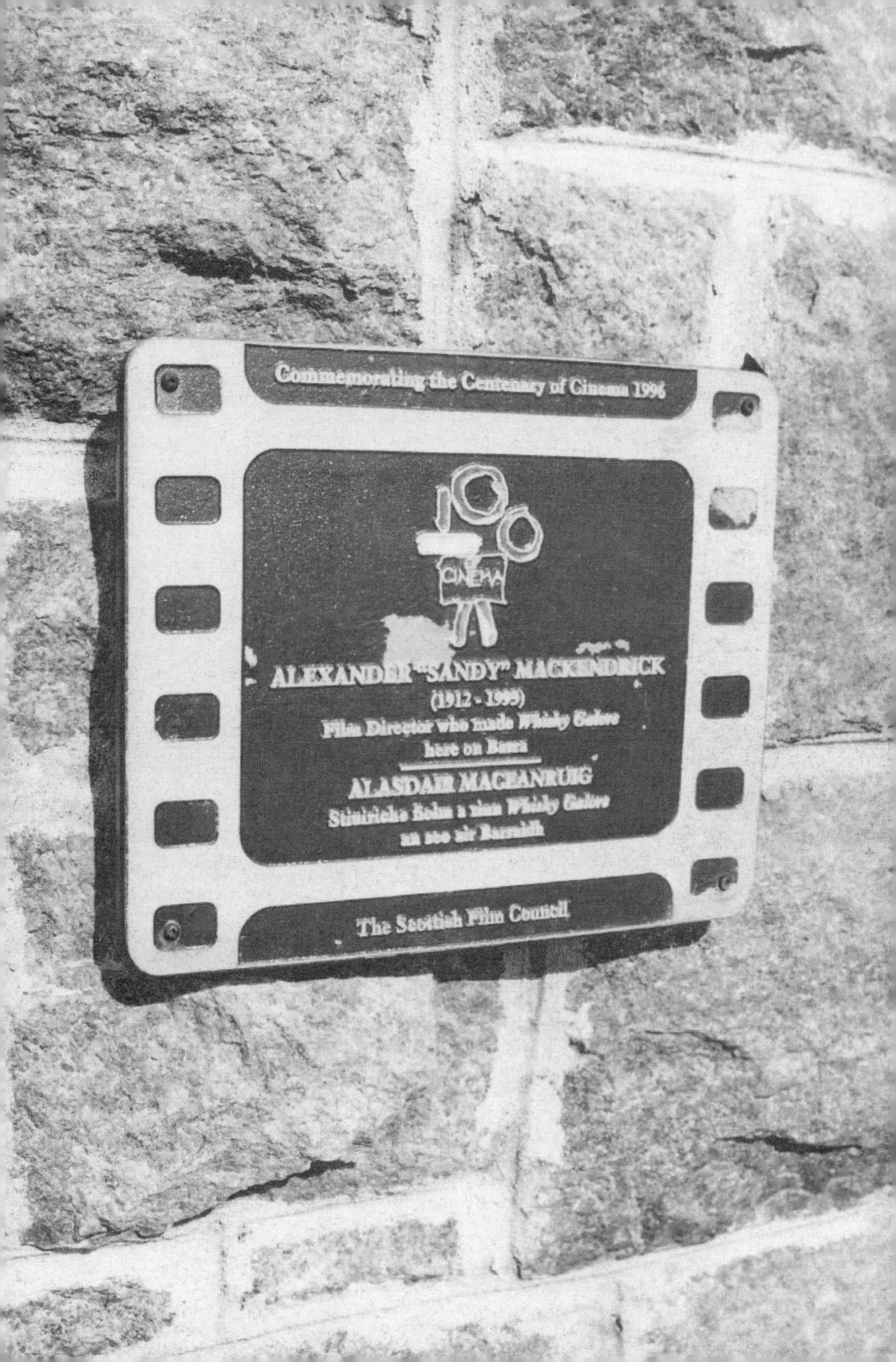
Commemorating the Centenary of Cinema 1996
CINEMA
ALEXANDER "SANDY" MACKENDRICK
(1912 - 1993)
Film Director who made Whisky Galore
here on Barra
ALASDAIR MACEANRUIG
The Scottish Film Council

future, but today we cared only for the moment. The tide was way out, and just visible between small rocky islets. Strangely, it seemed muddy out there. But perhaps this was an optical illusion made by the rare sight of seaweed.

Eventually we sat in a row, leaning against the car park fence, basking in the sun, sipping tea with the shore to our immediate front and telling each other what a heck of a bunch we were. Socks and shoes were removed. Kesh began to snore and Ram lay flat out, like some dangerous animal that you would do well not to step on.

'We call this Barra Heaven?' grinned Suk, delighted with himself. His wish to communicate his luck, together with word play, had all the sincerity of a happy boy.

'You guys the Gurkhas?' came a Gaelic voice. This was the airport's ground controller, the fellow with the ping pong ball bats, and as it transpired, not long discharged from our boys' current regiment, The Highlanders. Aged about forty, Jim was a tall, trim figure in blue coveralls. The boys exchanged names of mutual friends and shot the breeze, awaiting the incoming flight.

'He's teaching us – what do you call it – Gaelic!' confided Suk to Ewen.

Barra is almost completely Gaelic-speaking, and, endearingly, considers the likes of Stornoway to be far away and out of touch. The folk of the Highlands and Islands were a monoglot people who cherished their language, ennobled by a splendid oral culture. Gaelic is particularly suited for describing emotion, suffering, distance and nostalgia. Its speakers tend to use striking forms of expression unthinkingly.

When one mother bade farewell to her emigrant daughter in 1890, her words were naturally dramatic: 'This is our parting in this world. We must accept that we shall not be together until we meet before His Throne in Eternity.' The daughter, understandably, remembered every syllable. It rings down the years to us. On another occasion, a son remembered his mother's words at reading the black-edged telegram that bore the news of her husband's First World War death: 'The binding-tie has broken off our home.' Poetic, even in circumstances that would have the rest of us lost for words.

The Society for Propagating Christian Knowledge, established in 1707, initially forbade its teachers from using Gaelic but later realised the futility of its policy and began to publish religious books in the language. Among its publications were the New Testament, 1765, and the Old Testament, 1801. Until the beginning of the Nineteenth Century the majority of the islanders could not read or write but when the Edinburgh Gaelic Schools Association sent teachers to the Isles, and actually built schools, the level of literacy rose at an astonishing speed.

The newly literate enjoyed studying the Bible at home and communities organised prayer meetings at which passages from Focal Dhè (God's Word) were read aloud. It is interesting, though, to realise how emigrants always wrote home in English. This dates to the 1872 replacement of the Gaelic Society Schools by Board Schools in which English held sway.

Gaelic was always seen as an obstruction to integration and subjugation by the south and to this day it cannot be used in court. Until recently had you addressed an envelope using the Gaelic spelling of place names the Royal Mail was perfectly within its rights to throw it away.

Right up until the early part of the twentieth century it was customary for Registrars of Births and Deaths to refuse to enter Gaelic names in their registers. In Gaelic-speaking families, one of the most popular girl's names is Oighrig (pronounced in Lewis as ay-rig, or in Uist as uyee-rig), yet it was constantly transcribed as Henrietta or Euphemia. Strangely, in modern times, Erica, an Anglicised form of Oighrig, has become popular. The fact that Erica is the botanical name for heather may help explain the current popularity for Heather as a personal name too.

The 1891 Census showed there were 254,415 Gaelic speakers, whereas today there are about 80,000 with 23,500 of these in the Western Isles. No matter its beauty, the language seems doomed. There is a Nepalese parallel; just as my mother cannot speak the Gaelic of her great grandparents, similarly the modern Gurkha is today losing the old

Overleaf. ***Left:*** **Captain Dhal checks the undercarriage.**
Right: **Our aviators anticipating take off.**

PIPER

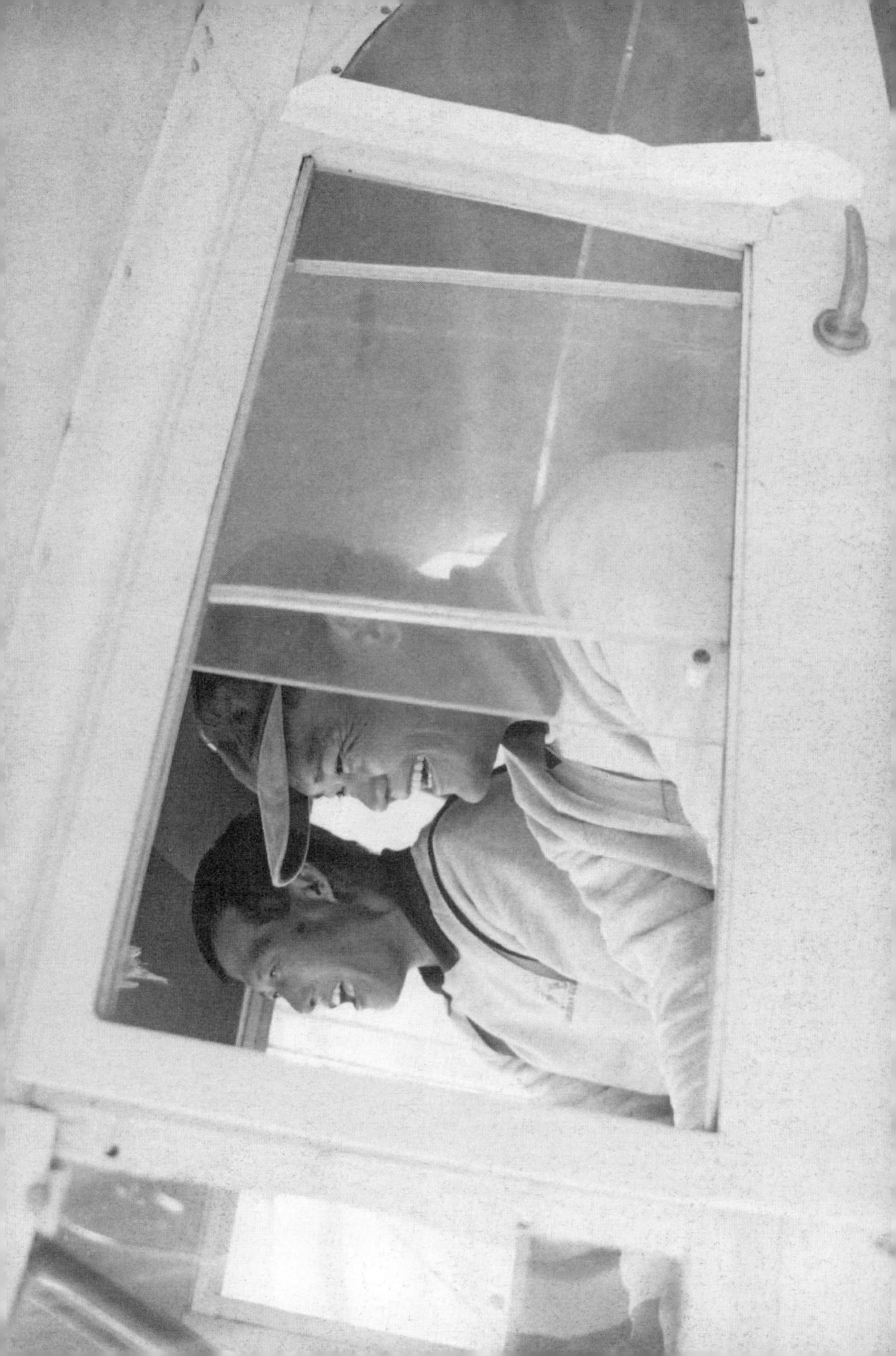

languages of his grandparents as the national universality of Nepali grows.

Our boys were never going to get further than 'madainn mhath', 'good morning'. Suk and Nugendra practised on each other but we'd have to wait until breakfast to see if they could remember it.

I phoned Simon Pia at the *Scotsman*: 'We're sitting on one of the most beautiful beaches in the world, the sky is cloudless and we're feeling a million dollars.'

'Heard about your salmon poaching on Radio Scotland!' chided Simon.

'Yeah, sorry about that. The story sort of grew before I could tell you.' I'm a shameless liar. 'How did Radio Scotland cover it?'

'Oh, that was in the newspaper review. Bit of a giggle. I've got the piece in front of me.' *The Record* had not put our address at the bottom but it seemed fair and funny and would certainly lift our profile but without the corresponding financial response. The headline read 'Gurkha Fish Gaffe'.

We cooked up a tale about our television appearance and discovering our Barra nirvana.

'Got to go, the plane's coming in!'

The small silhouette flew low from our left, the east, and before we knew it the British Airways' Twin Otter was bouncing straight towards us on big black tyres, its propellers spinning and engines revving. In a moment there was total silence as a handful of visitors climbed down the neat staircase with the dignity of hens emerging from the hutch, straight on to the sand and up towards the terminal. The papers came tumbling out of the hold, not in a square parcel but in a big roll. Apparently these were about to be rushed to Castlebay for distribution. Media executives were, we were led to believe, already straining at their leases.

We only waited for a few minutes before Jim was directing the pilot to re-start the engines. Another clutch of passengers trooped out and boarded. The doors shut, the aircraft took off for Glasgow and the whole process was complete until the next day.

The reversion to a blank silence, made drowsy by the heat, was like another switch had been thrown.

This part of the Isle was a long thin isthmus and the Atlantic was behind us, hidden by dunes. I got to my feet and headed off alone for about four hundred yards, crossing a machair so thick with clover I was practically wading.

The sand was like crossing hot hills of talc, but then a cool breeze hit my nostrils and suddenly there before me was the biggest, whitest seashore I'd ever seen. The beauty actually made my heart rate increase, as a wave of elation swept through me. This was practically a coral beach, and one of the world's finest, whose curtain had been unexpectedly raised by a mere two minute stroll. No wonder I was nearly reeling. The shore stretched out of sight, perhaps up to heaven, and the blue sea was broken only by long thin waves which splashed exuberantly on the sand. Instinctively, I ran back to shout to the others.

'Hey guys, ketaharu!' A couple of heads lifted from the clover. 'Hey, lads, come over here! Have a look at this!'

The figures came strolling over from their east-facing beach to the new one, Suk and Nugendra making slow-motion dives into the machair before they arrived between two towering dunes and the view ahead began to present itself.

'Wow, fantastic!' shouted Dhal, coming down a slope so white it looked like snow. That he was wearing walking boots only added to the illusion. Suk tobogganed down on his chest like a giggling otter. An onshore breeze cooled and invigorated, blowing away the sleepy indolence of minutes before. The seaward panorama was almost fictionally perfect; if the weather was like this more often they could have flown in Tilda Swinton and Leonardo DiCaprio to make *The Beach*, albeit *The Bracing Version*. This was a heroic beach.

Like high-spirited kids we all ran to the sea, howling and babbling. Like true summer holiday boys, when presented with huge open spaces we simply had to sprint about in them, rotating arms, leaping about, and simply expressing a vigorous affirmation of life. The only man-made artefact was a bizarre armchair made from polystyrene, whose expanded beads were only slowly being eroded. Suk and Kesh fell on it with gusto,

Overleaf. ***Left:*** **Barra Airport with Gurkhas.**
Right: **Penalty shoot out. Note our Piper aircraft on edge of beach.**

kicking it to pieces with a joyous determination that made you wonder if plastic chairs were a long-standing enemy and their due dispatch a traditional Gurkha duty.

The *Glasgow Herald* published my 2,000-word article on this trek (though removing all *Daily Record* references) and printed Dhal's picture on 'the snow' over most of the page. Suk's otter antics appeared alongside.

'You know something, guys, there are hardly any Scots who have been here,' I said.

For a moment Suk and Nugendra looked puzzled, as if wondering 'if not the Scots then who?' 'I mean hardly anyone has ever been here.'

'Dead right, and hardly any have seen it like this,' added Dhal.

I found myself reciting (though some was an unintentionally personalised version): 'Much have I travelled in the realms of gold/ And many goodly states and kingdoms seen;/ Round many western islands have I been/ which bards in fealty to Apollo hold.' I was indeed stout Cortez staring, not at the Pacific, but the Atlantic, and my Gurkhas did not look 'at each other with wild surmise'; they yelled with pleasure.

One man who had seen this area at its most breathtaking was Compton Mackenzie who lay buried at Eoligarry to our immediate north. Though born in West Hartlepool and lived mostly in Edinburgh's No. 31 Drummond Place, his heart was always in Barra. It was here between 1934 and 1936 that he wrote six books. He was Rector of Glasgow University and literary editor of the *Daily Mail* too. He also ran the Dickens Fellowship and was president of the Siamese Cat Club! Obviously, he, for one, did not find the Isle's remoteness a disadvantage. His nearby three-sided house, Suidheachan, the sitting-down place, was so-named because that's where the Macneil of Barra used to sit to have lunch when out snipe shooting.

The author died on St Andrew's Day 1972 and his coffin was flown in to our airstrip on a stormy December morning. I somehow think he would have approved of our lads and their undisguised happiness at sharing his Isles.

'Did he ever write about Gurkhas?' asked Nugendra.

'Like famous authors like what I am? No, In fact the only book I can think of which mentions a Gurkha is Kipling's *The Man Who Would Be*

King. It's about two British soldiers who find a lost kingdom in the Himalaya. They form an army and one is mistaken for a god. They are helped by a Gurkha, a Gurung, in fact. It was made into a film too, with Michael Caine and Sean Connery. I'll get you a copy of the book if you want?'

'Can you get me one of your Nepali books too?' he wondered, meaning my pocket dictionary.

'You can get that yourself in any good bookshop, you big Gurungseni!'

'Gurungseni!' (Old Gurung woman) he grinned. 'Gurungseni!'

'Okay, boys, let's get back for some late lunch,' I declared like a worn-out dad who'd suddenly remembered he'd had hardly any sleep the night before and had walked over a hundred miles in the past few days.

Mid-afternoon we drove back into Castlebay but somehow the Western Isles' edition of the *Record* did not have our 'Gurkha Fish Gaffe' article. I phoned my colleague, Leigh Howieson, back in Edinburgh, from the harbour's edge. Leigh acted as an unpaid executive-relay-station, all-round-admin-centre and back-up department. Not only did she have the *Record*'s piece but had compiled a cuttings' library. And our 'poached salmon' story was the talk of the steamie back home, but that wasn't all. The report had even drawn queries from newspapers in Nepal. Though our sights hadn't been international, we'd succeeded in raising our profile in ways beyond expectation. Gurkhas were to come up to me for the next year telling me they'd read about us. Later Iain MacIver generously sent on his fee together with a video of all the filming from his cameraman.

'What's this castle?' asked Dhal, pointing with his thumb, Gurkha fashion, at Kisimul. Fortresses meant war, and war meant stories.

The stone stronghold stood like a square keep in the centre of the bay to which it had given its name. A castle had been here since castles had been invented and had long been the base of the Macneil clan. It had been reduced to a ruin in 1795 and the whole island sold to our old friend, Gordon of Cluny, in 1838 by General Macneil, the 41st Chief. He died in

Overleaf. *Left:* Dhal crosses the 'snow'.
***Right:* Suk pretends to be an otter.**

1863 and the line effectively ended. However, in 1915 Robert Lister of Canada proved his right to the chieftainship in the Court of the Lord Lyon in Edinburgh. An architect, he changed his name and acquired the whole of Barra in 1937. By the time he died most of the restoration work was completed. The present chief, Iain Macneil, had recently put it in the care of Historic Scotland for a 1,000-year lease and an annual rent of a single bottle of whisky. Not only that but he had read about Hebridean Gurkha in the papers and had sent us a big cheque.

When I imparted this information to Rab McNeil of *The Scotsman* he expressed outrage and vowed never to pay his clan subs ever again. Rab recently put to bed the rumour that he had once, after ten pints of Belhaven, signed up for the Brigade of Gurkhas. He wrote: 'Let me state enigmatically, I have never drunk ten pints of Belhaven Ale (though I have drunk 11) and I have never been further east than Dunbar. To me, Nepal is another country.' We reckoned there had been some confusion concerning his spell in the Women's Auxiliary Air Force. Unbelievably, the picture editor had taken a small group of Gurkhas at the remembrance parade to mark the King of Nepal's assassination and superimposed Rab's head on to that of Nugendra. This was a complete coincidence but I warned Rab that Nugendra might not be too pleased. 'Tell him that I'm now working in Greenland as *The Scotsman*'s walrus correspondent,' had been the desperate response.

The Macneil clan wasn't always so generous. General Macneil had built an alkali works on his island. To raise the capital he divided every croft into two halves but maintained the same rent for each. He quickly went bankrupt and 500 of his tenants emigrated as soon as he introduced the scheme. When Gordon of Cluny took over he transported any excess peasants to Canada whether they liked it or not.

'But, Neil, there are photos of hundreds of fish boats here. We saw them over there,' Suk indicated the Visitors' Centre. 'Why were they poor?' That there was widespread poverty in Britain at the height of the Empire was always confusing, nearly shocking, to my Nepalese.

'You're right. But it wasn't until the 1850s that Castlebay, Lochboisdale, Lochmaddy and Stornoway became major fishing ports,' I replied (all this was news to me until our visit to the Heritage Centre minutes before). 'Over 400 boats used Castlebay, mostly from the east coast of Scotland. The landlords wouldn't let any wealth grow here. Any driftwood on the beach was the landlord's property and they would search the houses to find it. If you improved your house, the rent went up, so no one could ever accumulate any money.'

'And what happened to the boats?'

'They wiped out the herring. Right now they are wiping out the sand eel for fishmeal. Conservation and fisher folk never mix.'

'There were hundreds of boats here?' said Nugendra, agog.

'Yeah, seems strange looking at it now, doesn't it?'

'They must have been strange.'

We drove back across the island, the sun still blazing on the cottage roofs. One old man, on his corrugated iron roof, stopped from his work of painting it bright red, to give us a friendly wave. He couldn't have known who we were; he was just a typical local.

'The slates round here are from Lancashire and Wales,' commented Campbell.

'How do you know all about slate?' Ewen asked, impressed.

'Oh, I know all about slate,' smiled Campbell. 'Before I was in the Army I was a slaterer.'

'In Nepal we are changing slates and putting in corrugated iron,' said Dhal. 'Slate is old fashioned.'

'What's your father's house like?' I suddenly wanted to know.

'Stone with carved wooden front,' he replied, smiling to himself at the memory.

It took two minutes lying on the hotel bed before I began drifting off. Only four o'clock but sleep could not be resisted. Dhal and Ram were sitting in the sun outside, cleaning and playing their pipes, with an unfading energy. It crossed my mind that the hotel might object but then convinced myself they'd enjoy the repertoire. The air was full of the tangy, spangled music as if the notes had come home.

There was an important subject that was confusing me about the Isles:

Overleaf. *Left:* Me, apparently lost in the Sahara.
***Right:* Our Xanadu. Relaxing at Barra Airport.**

something called The Crofters' Holdings Act of 1886 which had created the UK's most unusual form of land tenure. Without knowing its history it is not possible to understand the Western Isles at all because it was land ownership, tenancy and eviction that had shaped the Hebrideans' whole mind set for hundreds of years. I produced my notebook and read it carefully.

The Act had come about as a direct result of the cruelty of the big landlords, such as the Gordons and Mathesons. Gladstone had set up the Napier Commission out of fear that Scotland was going to invent its very own Irish Land League but then appointed some apparently unsuitable commissioners.

Lord Napier himself owned 7,000 acres of valuable land in Selkirk, including Traquair and Thirlestane. The vested interests were further represented by Sir Kenneth Mackenzie of Ross and Cromarty, proprietor of 400,000 acres, who was joined by Donald Cameron of Locheil, possessor of 100,000 acres. But there were also cultural experts who included Charles Fraser-Mackintosh, Liberal MP for Inverness and Gaelic scholar, and Sheriff Alexander Nicolson, another well-known Gaelic scholar. There was also Professor Mackinnon, Chair of Celtic Studies at Edinburgh University. It might not appear so to our eyes but this was as eclectic a group as one was going to find in a 19th century commission.

They took evidence in Skye and then Barra, transcribing over a third of a million words of evidence from all groups of society with the directive to probe 'a state of misery, of wrong-doing, and of patient long-suffering without parallel in the history of our country.' This was a extraordinary stance for both government and fellow landowners, and for the 1880s represented an enormous humanitarian initiative.

The tales of hardship deeply moved the commissioners. The report described the degradations and sordid lives of the witnesses and also mentions their 'decency, courtesy, virtue and even mental refinement.' That many were giving evidence in a second language should remind us how educated was the average islander. The testimony is heart-breaking but also defiant. The tales of dispossession, fines and the constant intimidation and violence by the authorities reads like the Nazis in Poland.

The Crofters' Act eventually gave security of tenure to those who already had a croft and the right to claim compensation from the landlord for any improvements made. They were entitled to pass on their croft to their descendents and a Crofters' Commission was created to fix fair rents.

What the Act could not do was meet the howling hunger of the landless. Paupers and cottars were still in fear of the Poor Laws which were never meant to eradicate poverty. The Commission's biggest lasting failure was that despite the precise recommendations that the crofters' farming units be economic, the later Act disregarded the advice. The 7.5 acre size would be too small to live off, tenants would never be independent and always be beholden to their betters. It was a bitter barb that poisoned the whole exercise, but the Act was a big improvement on what had gone before.

Without it, though, it is possible that there would be no surviving crofting communities anywhere today – and probably no surviving Gaelic either. Arran, for example, was a Gaelic island a century ago, but was not included in the legislation. Today few regard Arran as part of Gaeldom; there is hardly one Gaelic native speaker on the Isle. This was the single most important Act to have hit the Isles and its benefits and shortcomings still affect life here. Not just the land and language were preserved but their very culture too.

Later we strolled across the brilliantly white beach outside in extended line and dark glasses like a very strange scene from *Reservoir Dogs*. Behind the hotel could be seen a couple of Highland cattle, gazing blindly through their shaggy fringes. We walked over. It seemed we couldn't let an hour pass without activity.

'What are these used for?' frowned Kesh.

'Mostly for their meat. They're a very old breed, so I expect they're used for breeding out defects in other breeds,' replied Ewen. 'You don't see many.'

'Are they, er, can you touch them?' Suk sought for the word 'tame'.

'I wouldn't if I was you.'

The long horns and matted coats obviously reminded them of home.

Overleaf. *Left:* The pipes are calling. Dhal in accustomed repose.
***Right:* Ewen takes in the scenery. Our hotel to his rear.**

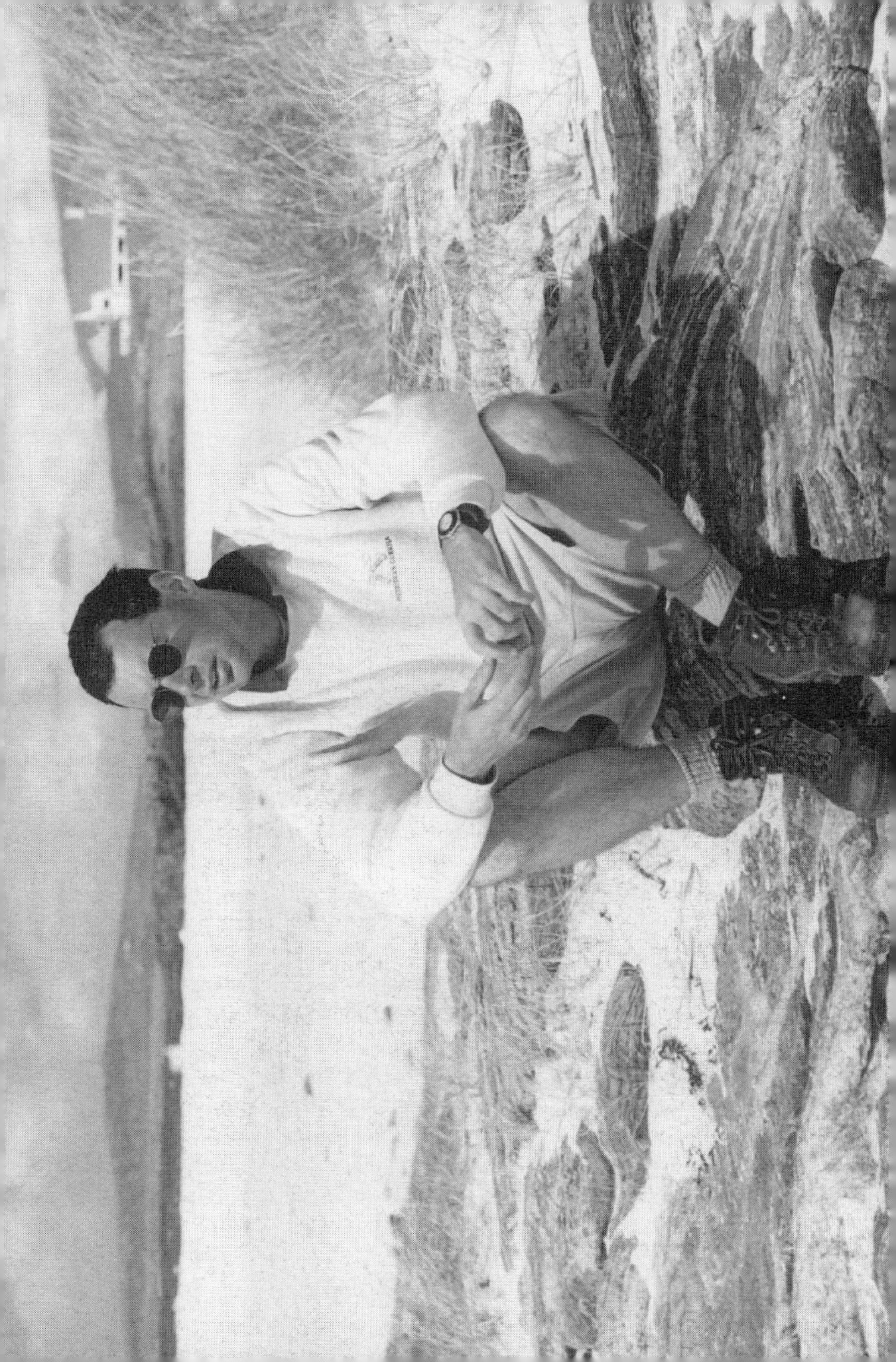

'How do you kill them?' Oh, great: the typical Gurkha question.

'Er, the normal way, I suppose. A bolt-gun to the forehead.'

'We suffocate yak,' said Dhal.

'You do what?'

'We suffocate them,' he repeated, proud either of the deed itself or knowing the verb. 'But we never kill white ones. Do you have white ones?'

'Perhaps, but I'm sure they're butchered too.' Sometimes our cultures are so similar but it's the small things that differentiate us.

At supper the late sun streamed through the huge glass wall that was the west end of the restaurant, half blinding us. The Atlantic outside was a black and gold splendour that art or Hollywood could only dream of mimicking. Gurkhas are naturally adventurous and their speculative choices of menu dishes often lead to disappointment. The minted lamb in South Uist had been a typical example – and was universally loathed – but tonight the lads plumped for the known; steak or fish. Yet again, the micro-ed vegetables let down the ensemble. Though the sense of adventure might have diminished, their love of stories seemed to grow.

'Neil, tell us a story about Barra,' asked Suk. 'A war one.'

'How about this? In the old days the warships of Barra, the longboats, under their chief took to raiding the English ships of Queen Elizabeth I. The Queen asked the Scottish King, James VI, to bring him to justice. The clan chief was tricked and captured and sent to Edinburgh under guard. At the trial before the King the chief claimed he had only attacked the English ships because the Queen had killed the King's mother. This was true, by the way. Mary Queen of Scots had been beheaded at Elizabeth's order.

'King James was so dumbfounded at this explanation, he allowed the chief to return to Barra but had to pay an annual fine of £40.'

'So he escaped?' Suk looked askance, 'Because the English Queen had killed the Scottish King's mother?' To the Gurkhas this didn't seem a very good deal. Surely, the King should have rewarded the Macneils, not fined them? It's just as well they didn't know about Elizabeth's privateers raiding the Spanish at the same time, for which the captains were knighted. History through Gurkha eyes always throws new light on old stories.

'Do you know why Nepal is called "a small kingdom with a high price"?' questioned Dhal. I had no idea that it had such a name but we nodded to let him continue. 'Prithvi Narayan Shah was crowned King of Gorkha in 1743. Then it was small country west of Kathmandu. When on a pilgrimage when he was fifteen, he looked at the valley of Kathmandu, Patan and Bhaktapur with Brahman astrologers. He decided he would one day rule it. He knew it was mad. There were not enough men in Gorkha and the valley was rich in men and money. The astrologers knew it was mad too, but knew what he was feeling in his heart, even though he didn't say anything. They said it will be a river of blood. They said: "Your voice frightens elephants!"' Dhal broke off to laugh, but he continued: 'In twenty-five years there was a river of blood but Prithvi Narayan had his small kingdom with a high price. And that's how we got our name.'

Campbell, who had been eating less than a Stornoway sparrow when we arrived and whose appetite had grown as his tan had deepened, cajoled: 'What about you, Suk? Any stories?'

Suk's eyebrows lifted. 'We are having a new OC, Major Naylor Saheb. When we were in Brunei, I was the company runner and in the jungle I broke his tea pot.'

'He had a tea pot in the jungle?'

'Oh yes, he had a teapot and I broke it. I am worried that he remembers.'

We all laughed. 'And that's your best story?' Suk shrugged ruefully, realising this wasn't exactly a classic folk story, but still provided a giggle. Our day, like his tale, was over.

CHAPTER SEVEN

BARRA HEAD

The boys were assembled at the hotel's reception desk, sitting by their luggage. As usual we were the first for breakfast but the lads were passing the time by chatting up the young female receptionist. 'Madainn mhath, Neil!' they greeted. The rotten cheats; the girl had just repeated the phrase for them.

'What do you usually have for breakfast at home?' she asked. There was the usual confab as to the correct English which sometimes gave the impression they didn't even know the answer to the simplest questions.

'Er, rolls and ghui?' replied Suk, looking at me for confirmation of the word.

'Ghee, yes, clarified butter, practically the same word. Though in Nepal it's usually buffalo butter.'

'Where are you boys goin' the day?' she asked.

'Joe McNeil is taking us on his boat to Barra Head, then tonight we're leaving for Oban.'

'Choe? I hope not, the poor man's got Alzheimers.'

'Um, well it's his boat. Let's hope it's his son!'

It was nine o'clock and breakfast was done. We were waiting in the cloudless sunshine beside the van awaiting the as yet unseen Campbell. Ewen and I knocked on his door.

'C'mon out! Leave that sheep alone and get out here!'

Opposite. Gurkhas at sea. It's calming, and so are we.

'Baa! Baa!' From within could be heard muffled declarations of innocence and that he thought we were leaving at ten.

'We're supposed to be leaving now. Our boat's leaving at ten.'

Campbell eventually walked out to the van to a round of applause and a chorus of sheep bleats. At that moment, Ewen and I were not exactly his favourite people.

At Castlebay we quickly found our vessel, a small boat with wheelhouse for'ard, a rear deck and an inflatable dinghy attached aft. On the slipway Campbell suddenly decided that he didn't want to go on the two hour eighteen-mile journey. It would be too rough. He felt unwell. Nobody listened and he was cheerfully bundled aboard as if the boys were an experienced press gang. I suspect that had he resisted more firmly, there might well have been a corresponding increase in their firmness.

The boatman, Donald, looked about thirty-five and had with him an elderly relation. There was also a cousin, aged about thirty, looking out of place in our remote surroundings with shaved head and earring. The boys sat around the rear not really knowing what was ahead. We were literally all in the same boat.

'The Gurkhas become Marines,' I said light-heartedly, as the engine started up. 'The night we went to Birmingham by way of Barra Head.' For a few minutes the vessel made steady unexciting progress as it crossed the big bay. Then we hit the swell where the shelter of Barra and Vatersay disappeared.

'Wow!' yelled Dhal as we chugged up one wave and then crashed down the other side, the dinghy sliding behind us, with salt water exuberantly gushing over our low sides. The freeboard was scarcely two feet and this could only be the beginning of a real to-your-bones soaking. Every time we crashed into a trough, seated Gurkhas were thrown into the air while those standing at the rear stumbled and banged into each other. The immediate ascent up the next wave saw them all regroup in an involuntary drunken shuffle and the process began all over again. Surely this couldn't last for two hours there and two hours back, could it? What if it got worse? This was a perfect day's weather, wasn't it? Above us the blue sky was blown through with lively small clouds which augured badly. 'Hey ho, me hearties,' Ewen roared, as he staggered one way and then another.

The old man grinned at our drunken sailor antics. The exhilaration of a helter-skelter on the high seas with a bit of a big dipper thrown in was unexpectedly wild. It was at this point, with us going up and down like yoyos on a trampoline, that the old man asked if we wanted a cup of tea.

'Tea! How're we gonna drink it?' hooted Suk. But Campbell, who had missed breakfast, nodded and had a big plastic cup handed to him. The man re-appeared from the wheelhouse with a huge kettle and poured the tea into the proffered cup with an expertise that only comes with a lifetime at sea. We watched in fascination as the ballet came to its conclusion: the milk and then several spoons of sugar from a bag of Tate & Lyle's granulated. Nothing went awry until Campbell lifted it to his mouth.

'Ah, ah, ah ah, ah!' The hot liquid flushed out both nostrils in one scalding moment of inattention. It would be an utter travesty to say: my, how the chaps chuckled.

I moved up to the wheelhouse and the shaven-headed guy pointed at a line of birds flying nose to tail in a long chain. 'Puffin,' he said. 'I've eaten puffin. Very tasty, but they take ages to boil.' I didn't like this guy at all. 'I'm Kenny. That's Bob,' he indicated the old fellow. Inevitably, we began talking and within minutes I was wondering why I'd prejudged him so fiercely. Kenny worked in television, and was a local but based in Glasgow. It was no surprise that a Gaelic-speaker with an arts degree who worked in the media was mostly involved in Gaelic TV. We had a number of mutual acquaintances. Ewen and he shared some too. This was a man bursting with local history and gossip and could tell us a lot.

'That's Vatersay over there. The most southerly of the Outer Hebrides to be inhabited. When they created the Western Isles Council in 1975 the first thing they did was build some council houses. Except they forgot to put in fireplaces. They were all electric in a land surrounded by peat! And as the power comes from South Uist there are plenty of power cuts. The folk down here reckon everyone in Stornoway is a self-serving moron.'

We described the trek so far. 'The boys were fascinated by the *Whisky Galore!* story most. Eriskay, though, was a bit of a disappointment.'

Overleaf. *Left:* Water, water everywhere. Like acres of ruffled sappire.
***Right:* Ascent into heaven. We leave the boat behind.**

ROLLING

'It was for Bonnie Prince Charlie too. It was where he first landed in Scotland. We don't know exactly what he did there. One story has him grilling flounders and another has him staying with the tacksman who didn't know who he was. The beach where he's supposed to have landed is still called Coilleag a' Phrionnsa – the Prince's Strand. A plant is supposed to grow there which grows nowhere else. Charlie had scattered some special seeds from his pocket. Aye right.'

'Magic beans,' I laughed.

Gaels and Gurkhas are compulsive story-tellers but I think only the former improve on the truth. The Nepalese enjoy utter fantasy but don't, as a rule, embroider the facts. They like the unvarnished, often brutal truth, rarely equivocate and seem incapable of lying.

Our journey was settling down. The drunken sailor act had stopped as the sea calmed. Ram's squat figure had been thumping up and down on the bench so much that I feared he might end up an inch or two shorter.

'Ram, how tall are you?'

'Five foot two,' he grinned. The Gurkha minimum height, I thought (though it was increased by an inch in 2004). Ram had remained entirely self-contained for the duration of our trek, never moaned and hardly said anything. While there was no doubt he was enjoying himself, I wondered what was going on in his cropped head.

The sea was a rippling blue, torn through with blazes of white foam spread with sparkling handfuls of sunlight. Oh yes, Suk was right: this was heaven.

Sandray was now on our starboard bow. The Isle was evacuated in the 1930s. Ahead lay the rising form of Mingulay. This is only 1.5 miles by 2.5 miles across but is home to some of Britain's biggest cliffs which tore a sheer 700 feet out of the Atlantic on Creation Day and only just remembered to stop. The eastern side had been inhabited for centuries but it too was evacuated in the 1930s. It holds a special place in the hearts of the people of Barra.

'See these?' asked Bob. 'This iss my grandmother and her wee brother on Mingulay. About 1900.' The picture showed a very good-looking girl aged about fourteen. Wearing a white dress with a stylish élan, her hair was tousled, long and dark, while her bare feet completed what looked like an ethnic fashion shoot. She looked directly into camera with supermodel poise. There was even an accompanying urchin who looked suspiciously like he'd been supplied by the props department.

'My family was from Mingulay,' he said proudly.

'Ah, I remember this island!' I exclaimed, spotting the abandoned village on the edge of the bay. Knowing I'd never been in the Isles before, Ewen looked enquiringly. 'There was a film about the Royal family. The Royal Yacht dropped anchor here and they went ashore and met some female artist who was living here for a year.'

'That's right,' said Kenny. 'Can't remember her name, but I saw it too. In fact, there was somebody else who stayed here for a year too. The highest peak is called Macphee's Hill after a rent collector that arrived here to discover everyone had died of the plague and they wouldn't let him back on the rowboat in case he infected them. They left him for a year!'

'Aye, but the Macneil gave him land in compensation,' added Bob loyally. 'You know, he would always find you a new cow if your old one died. Or a wife.'

'Which ever was the most important!' I put in.

He beamed back. 'Aye, aye,' he concurred slowly, as if he'd personally known the old chief.

The boat pulled into the bay, the bright sand below making it seem only a few feet deep. We clambered up to the bows as the engine cut and we drifted nearer the shore.

'Look at how clear!' Kesh in the bowsprit held out his arms to show their shadows on the seabed below; even his fingers could be seen.

'Over there on the left was the only proper landing stage; they used a sort of crane for the heavy stuff,' pointed Kenny.

'Aw naw, the chapel roof has fallen in,' said Bob with a moan. This, we were led to believe, was a serious blow. It had stood since the 1880s and represented a link in stone to a lost past. Its collapse was an emotional moment of passage. 'We'll haff to tell everyone,' Bob groaned, as if this

Overleaf. *Left:* Summit of achievement. The boys enjoy the moment.
***Right:* Nugendra was blown away by the view.**

responsibility was another burden.

The engine restarted and we headed for our final destination, Barra Head, over a sea that resembled nothing more than acres of ruffled sapphire. There was a tiny quay which our boat edged into with calm precision. The leap ashore required equal confidence, as the landing was slippery with seaweed.

'Right, guys, we've got about a mile to walk, up there to the lighthouse, have lunch and come back.'

The moment must have inspired them because the lads shot off as if supercharged. Kenny, Campbell and I strolled up in their wake, the white spire on the skyline reminiscent of a Buddhist gompa. The climb was only 680 feet but the heat, accumulated fatigue and the fact that I was wearing jeans instead of shorts combined to make this tougher than expected. If Kenny had wanted a demonstration as to how quickly Gurkhas can move, he got one today.

As we climbed, the line of Isles stretching to our north was laid out in the sun as if we were flying. Mingulay, Pabbay, Vatersay and Barra lay like grazing beasts behind us. I was right, few will have ever seen the sights encountered by the Hebridean Gurkhas and even fewer in these happy conditions.

'Was this ever inhabited?' Campbell wondered, looking at our empty valley.

'Oh yeah, and was the first bit of Scotland sighted by Bonnie Prince Charlie,' began Kenny.

'Oh, great, that man again! Can we ever escape him? We go to the end of the world and guess who's been here?' I commented. 'What was that about a plague on Mingulay? I thought the Western Isles were famous for not having plagues?'

'Well, we don't really know what happened in Mingulay but it's true that the Isles rarely had big outbreaks of disease,' explained Kenny. 'They had some. The occasional smallpox and so on but as soon as they got to Glasgow they all came down with TB, so that people credited their good health to the black houses, believe it or not. There was a terrible TB that hit the Isles in the 1920s – probably came back with the troops. It was known as 'an caitheamh', the wasting. The poor sods were put in isolated ruins. Kids were not allowed to play in the ruins. They're still not!'

'So the black houses didn't produce even a resistance?' Campbell asked.

'No, we didn't have plagues because we were just isolated, that's all. There was an enteric disease that came from byres being stored with dung and human excrement. When it was spread on the fields in the spring they came down with 'dung fever' – galair an todhair. But that was just about it – apart from the occasional diphtheria.'

'When did people leave the black houses? It must have been recent?'

'In the 1930s. Young couples began to realise the danger to their babies' health and moved out. With no windows, the atmosphere inside was always choking with smoke. Quite a few had worked as maids in Glasgow and they even tried to introduce wallpaper!' Kenny's expertise was substantial and he enjoyed sharing it.

'Think I'm gonna stop here,' announced a breathless Campbell. There was no arguing this time, so Kenny and I hurried on our way. The summit could only be ten minutes away. The goal of seven day's walking beckoned.

At last I could put my hand on the lighthouse. The idle whim to walk the length of the Outer Hebrides had come good. We had marched across the low brooding moors of Lewis, tramped across the rocky passes of Harris. We'd slogged through North Uist, and across Benbecula before hitting the sumptuous beaches of South Uist. We'd rested our bones in sand-ringed Barra and now stood contemplating the Atlantic at the Hebrides' most southerly point. Here the land really did meet the sea, and ran unstoppably into the sky somewhere in the distant blue. Looking out at the far horizon, I felt almost spiritually, not just at the end of my journey, but at one of the ends of the earth. There was a dreamy hazy quality to the view, it was utterly beautiful too.

The lighthouse had stood here since 1833, its white body capped by huge lenses and a dark metal dome. Suk and Nugendra were sitting near

Overleaf. *Left:* Dhal and Ram exchange congratulations. In the background: Mingulay, Pabbay, Vatersay and Barra.
***Right:* Three delighted Gurkhas exuding achievement.**

the cliffs, gazing at the near 700 foot drop while Kesh and Ram were resting on a small lawn. Dhal was slurping from a celebratory can of McEwans. We had done it. The air was practically shiny and split by dozens of whirling guillemots and puffins who were excitedly chasing each other round our summit at head height. The last thing they were expecting was a group of people, and constantly ran the risk of smashing straight into one of us. Knocked unconscious or even killed by a puffin would have been the least likely way to end our trip, but it was suddenly a dangerous possibility. 'He died when struck by a puffin' would lack a certain gravitas when appended to a gravestone.

'Hey, Neil, namaste!' greeted Dhal.

'Celebration time, ketaharu! Gather round. Kenny'll take our photos,' I said, producing the string of Buddhist prayer flags I'd bought in Ullapool along with a big green flag bearing the crossed kukris. 'Ram, see if you can find a pole and we'll prop these dhoza up above us.'

Seconds later Ram reappeared with a sixteen-foot length of scaffolding which he handled with determined intent.

'Ram! That's miles too big!'

'All there is,' he said flatly.

'Okay, let's anchor down the dhoza with some stones instead or they'll fly away.'

After countless photos (Kenny had to use eight cameras, each one at least twice), it was time to luxuriate in our achievement. The cliffs around us went straight down and continued to a horrible depth before they hit the seabed. There were no shallows here. After severe gales small fish are found where we now lay.

The puffins seemed half tame, as if they'd never seen humans before, but ignored our tempting morsels of sandwich as if they couldn't see us. Nugendra seemed particularly moved by the view while Kesh and Ram kept their impressive calm. Dhal and Suk just grinned.

It was with the sadness of knowing that we'd never return to such a magnificent eyrie, that we headed back down to our private cruiser. Spirits were high and we descended as if we were coming in to land from high above. The boat waited in water so clear it appeared to be floating on air – like us. Today we were in another realm.

Donald, the boatman, did not retrace our route but headed west out to the Atlantic. The immediate concern that this might mean a rougher trip was forgotten as the sight of a hundred seals diving into the sea from the rocks of Barra Head transformed the soldiers into excited camera-totting schoolboys. Moving slowly, we rounded the enormously high headland of Mingulay which soared into the sky above us. God's own North Atlantic defence. It resembled a massive meteorite, black and menacing but a source of total awe.

Once on Mingulay's Atlantic side Donald took us within a few feet of the enormous gneiss wall in a bravura piece of boatmanship. So close, we could not appreciate its towering height. The ocean was a deep aquamarine flecked with the brightest surf you ever saw – and it was immeasurably deep. There was a terrible sense of being on the edge of the world. America was somewhere on our left but helplessly far away. I imagine an astronaut on a spacewalk would know the feeling – floating free, far from home and suddenly vulnerable.

The boat pulled back so that we could take in the cliffs' majestic height. They stretched up and up. I could pick out some climbing routes but they spiralled so high that after the first 500 feet I was guessing. These were, of course, about the highest cliffs in Britain; their size should be no surprise.

Guillemots popped and dived around us but the air was filled with seabirds: shags, fulmars, puffins, kittiwakes and the odd gannet. Above us they flew in casual elegance or flapping frantic squadrons, all in different directions and speeds; an air traffic controller's nightmare.

'We call gannet Mingulay duck,' said Kenny. Both Bob and Donald nodded in agreement as if this were a confidence. 'If you effer handle razorbills without gloves, you'll soon find how they get their name. They've a special hook on their bill to rip you to pieces!'

The vessel turned unexpectedly into a narrow inlet and then turned right again. We slowly entered an immense flooded cathedral whose basalt

Overleaf. *Left:* We are sailing. The Gurkhas become Marines again. *Right:* Mingulay. Its cliffs are way beyond normal. This is God's own North Atlantic defence.

vaults soared above us, where seals gawped from the rocky lady chapels like generals interrupted during a sauna. We were in a David Attenborough film. In a week of the year, it was the day of the week: the time of our lives. Our necks had never been so craned.

We then edged our way out of the cave by another exit. Clearly, these visits were only rarely possible. We must have had all our gods watching over us.

Donald kept us on the western route and we headed home. Bob, it transpired, had worked with the Northern Lighthouse Board all his life. We shared the same boss, Admiral Sir Michael Livesay, and I was immediately but erroneously attributed all sorts of nautical skills. This was compounded when I used my GPS to read our speed. His eyes nearly popped out.

Bob still wanted to share the secrets of Mingulay: 'It has no peat, you know. They took it from Barra. And cod liver oil for lights. My grandmother, Mairì Mhòr wass a skilled brewer of ale. She wass recognized as the best stacker of barley and oats in the neighbourhood!'

Dhal asked: 'Did she do the threshing?'

'Oh, threshing wass always women's work.' He and Dhal grinned at each other. 'The first threshing machine came in the last summer before World War Two.'

When we tied up at Castlebay, its low hills and wide harbour now familiar, we noticed that the sea around the slipway was filled with about a hundred dead edible crabs that had been accidentally dropped whilst unloading. The Isles are surrounded by fish and prime lobster which are ferried all over Europe. Strangely, there is no tradition of excellent seafood restaurants here though – another Hebridean mystery.

The gang walked up to the Craigard Hotel, a long pale building set immediately below the Our Lady, Star of the Sea Church. Kenny came too, with a couple of friends we'd met outside the general stores on Main Street where we'd bought the postcards the day before. Anguished expressions crossed their faces to hear about the Mingulay chapel roof.

'*Whisky Galore!*' pointed Suk at the plaque, his white teeth flashing.

'Oh my God!' groaned Kenny. 'We had to watch that every year as children.' It turned out he was an expert on the film. 'It was a time they all still talk about. The wettest summer ever. 1949, and it was his first time as a director. Cast of eighty including Gordon Jackson, Duncan Macrae and James Robertson Justice.'

'Oh, yes, he played the doctor,' said Ewen. 'He was from the same village as my father. They used to go fishing together.'

'Ah, he actually did all his work at Pinewood but visited Barra during the filming. It was initially considered a disaster. Annoyingly, a French company, Canal Plus, now owns the rights, along with all the Ealing comedies. They filmed *Rockets Galore!* here too, in 1957.'

'Maybe *Gurkhas Galore!* soon!' giggled Suk.

Everyone sat on the long verandah outside the hotel, drinking tea and taking in the glorious view. We had been exposed to such sustained beauty that we couldn't over-enthuse but sat in a state of sated contentment. Ewen and I had really caught the sun, while Campbell was grateful we'd ignored his wish to stay ashore.

Nugendra commented on how much litter and garbage we'd seen, especially the big stuff like cookers. 'See that cliff over there? We used to drive all our old cars off it. There was nowhere else. Now there're laws which mean we pay a bomb to get rid of them.'

It was five o'clock and there was nothing to do until the 9.15 p.m. ferry, except have supper – or have a pint. Kesh and I wandered into the bar. The Friday afternoon drinkers, porky on their bar stools, gave us those sidelong looks that are not supposed to be seen, nodded to each other and, speaking in the Gaelic, told their neighbour we were Gurkhas. I know this because the Language of Eden uses the word 'Gurkha' and it now reverberated around the room.

Kenny left us, warning that the quicker we ordered supper the better. The Feis was about to start. This was the proper name for the music festival whose advance party we'd run into in the Uists. 'Even the bar staff'll be wrecked,' he said cheerfully. He departed with his pals and we lost both a guide and a friend.

The supper confirmed our opinion of the local cuisine. Beautiful North Atlantic prawn – a type of languistine – but served unappetisingly with boiled potatoes and frozen peas. We were half way through the meal when I was aghast to see the big Oban ferry steaming into the bay.

'Argh! What's that doing there?' I yelped. Ewen and I ran down to the harbour but the ferry offices were closed. Typical Hebrides! Just when you're getting to admire the laid-back lifestyle, its disadvantages are suddenly rammed home. There seemed no one either remotely interested or authoritative to ask. There was no notice board which might inform passengers and we were becoming angry in the absence of any explanation. Noticing the Port Authority office was open we pushed open the door and asked what was going on.

'No, that's not the Oban ferry. The Oban ferry has broken down and a replacement will dock between midnight and 1 a.m.,' we were told by two pleasant looking guys over big brown china mugs of tea. Did we really have to go this far to learn what was straightforward but important information, to wit, the departure time of our vessel? Not the end of the world, but annoying as hell. We were not on the promised ship but something brought out of mothballs. We'd have to hang around too. And what time would we get into Oban?

'No need to panic, guys, eat your meal slowly, we've got at least and extra three hours to wait,' I explained. No one was even slightly bothered.

Suk was thrilled to show me two discoveries he'd made. In one alcove, behind glass, was a bottle of whisky from the *SS Politician*, and on another wall was a big black and white print of a scene from the film being shot on the hill behind. They had built a corner of a house with a floor and two walls complete with windows and curtains but no ceiling. Natural light together with a huge arc lamp filled a shot of a couple at a table while in the background lay our old friends, Main Street and Kisimul Castle.

The noise from the bar was growing steadily with each passing minute, and young drinkers could be seen staggering around like they were learning to skate. When the bill was paid the pretty waitress smiled, declaring: 'Gurkhas, you'll always be welcome here,' which visibly delighted the lads. She then endeared herself by showing bafflement when I asked for a proper bill. 'What, like from the till?' she frowned, as if we had let her down. We were, after all, nothing more than a bunch of fussy mainlanders and I was Mr Pecksniff.

After walking round the block, i.e. the entire village, in an agreeable ramble, we realised that our road had run out. We did what all soldiers do with a few spare hours to kill; everyone fell asleep in the vehicle.

Just after one we drove on to the ferry and quickly found it was far from the luxury cruiser once envisaged. Nobody seemed worried. All the passengers found themselves in a small lounge and there were not even enough seats for everyone. Nugendra and I simply lay down beside each other on the carpet and fell asleep. A bit of discomfort wasn't going to throw any of us.

When I awoke it was 6 a.m. and we were in the Sound of Mull. The ship had clearly not been prepared for passengers and there was no café, but, I suppose, we were lucky to have a ferry at all. All the same, this didn't stop me wanting a cup of tea, and I went on the prowl like a hungry predator. This was a ship, and it had to have a cup of tea somewhere. I found an unlocked galley and quickly made myself a cuppa without a qualm. Not my usual behaviour but nothing seemed normal on this trip. Should this be called initiative or theft? Should I leave 50p or would it be discovered by some ne'er do well who'd simply pocket it? Legally speaking, I should deduct at least 30p for my labour.

Nugendra and I were standing at the bows. It was freezing and very clear. 'You've got a long leave coming up. What will you do with five months?' Nugendra had proved a dependable conscientious colleague as his plans showed. 'I want to do three things. An English course, learn to drive and learn how to do a PowerPoint presentation.'

'Marry?'

He gave a wan smile. 'Maybe.'

A passing deckhand stopped to say hello. 'Knew I'd meet up with you. We've all been keeping our eyes open for you.'

Oban was absolutely dead at 7 a.m. and truckers had told us the only place for breakfast was at the Crianlarich railway station. We stopped there to surprise a sleepy snackbar staff with an order for eight coffees and eight bacon rolls. The morning light shone on the surrounding pine forests like a tourist film and we moved the chairs on to the platform to eat in the

Overleaf. *Left:* The Magnificent Seven. We'd achieved all our targets. *Right:* Our trusty support vehicle below. Our Lady, Star of the Sea, Catholic church, Castlebay.

sunshine as swallows swooped back and forth from their nests above us.

By now I was completely familiar with the affectionate attention my friends brought but never took for granted the privilege of their company. The British Army has only 3,500 Gurkhas and it seemed that Ewen, Campbell and I were now honorary friends of all of them. Our eventual total was to reach £60,000 which would provide all the then 12,000 former Gurkhas or widows with a week's pension. The symmetry was coincidental but no less sweet and my colleagues blazed with pride to have been part of the achievement. Theirs is a community that reveres the elderly, and no one respects old Gurkha soldiers more than young Gurkha soldiers. The debt of honour was being repaid and it brought great happiness to the participants, the Brigade of Gurkhas and, of course, the eventual beneficiaries. The money goes straight to Nepal where the British MoD pays admin costs and the cash goes directly to the needy under the auspices of former Gurkhas with impeccable records. The donations could not be more effectively spent. A £5 per week pension isn't much, even in Nepal, but it is a constant wonder how it can provide subsistence for a whole family. Above all, the £5 per week and other benevolent payments tell these folk that Britain has not forgotten them. Unfortunately, when the recipient dies the loss of pension can be catastrophic for his household. There are other schemes, such as bridge-building, fresh water provision or even medical aid, which have an equally profound impact on communities leading some of the toughest existences on the planet.

It is these hill villages that produce the young Gurkha, a man inured to hardship, whose shoeless childhood in the thin air of his native mountains has hardened him for anything, and who understands the importance of family, friends and allies for survival. He will be faithful to all of them and if the loyalty is returned it will last a lifetime. The merry sons of Nepal are our oldest and best allies, who have stood alongside us since 1815 and asked for almost nothing except that they be respected. Their natural courtesy and dignity marks them out as gentlemen as well as gentle men, and if we make too much of this, it is because it is a virtue rare in this world. Britain has had many allies over the past 200 years and almost all have altered their relationship as national interests similarly changed. Not so the Gurkhas, they have remained unquestioningly pro-Britain even in times when perhaps we didn't deserve their unfailing service. From the Indian Mutiny, to Flanders mud, the Burmese jungle and the Falklands, the Gurkhas have come along with us, bearing their immense packs with a universal smile and ready to die in our cause. It is as much for his grin as his proud service that Britain loves the Gurkhas. 'Oh, they're always smiling,' is easily the most common recollection of those that know or even half-know the Nepalese fighting man.

And there's the rub. Despite his warm human nature, he has been employed by the Crown for his steadiness under fire and his cold courage. Though these combine to produce a unique soldier, there will always be an enigma at the heart of the wee men that will grow as we in the West grow away from the bloody reality of war. The Gurkha sees the way of the warrior as a noble calling, not a mere career choice, and in this he is more in tune with the soldier sahibs of the British Empire and Victorian society itself. The British may respect its Army but it no longer reveres soldiers per se, and finds killing any enemy as big a moral challenge as military. This is not the Gurkha way. He is neither stupid nor squeamish and tends to sort out problems the quick way. Soldiering is an honoured profession and has been for thousands of years as far as he's concerned. That others equivocate means that he will beat them in battle. Ayo Gurkhali! The Gurkhas are coming!

The Outer Hebrides had proved itself 'a part of the main' in its shared love of the men from the high Himalaya. The level of generosity we had encountered had been enormous and spirited. While our route had facilitated donations, there was no denying the islander's generosity; a shower of money had been pressed into our hands every day. The *Stornoway Gazette* was to reproduce the Barra Head team picture both as an over-sized accompaniment to my article and featured it on the masthead too. We were big news to these wonderful folk, but our biggest unifying factor was simple: both sides liked each other.

The Hebrides and Nepal had inched together over the brief week. Not

Overleaf. *Left:* The Gurkka Memorial outside the Ministry of Defence, Whitehall.
***Right:* Gurkhas Galore! The boys resting at Castlebay.**

only was there a shared love of the pipes and tartan, there was a shared military service stretching back over two hundred years. The men with the claymores had stood alongside the men with the kukris in the dust of the Khyber Pass and the Heights of Dargai, they'd seen action together at El Alamein and up the spine of Italy, and had tramped in step into Port Stanley. Nobody forgets those types of bonds.

But there was something more subtle about the cultural links. The shared love of storytelling and belief in the supernatural was obvious, but the Hebridean standing stones and Buddhist *mani* stones provided a forgotten similarity of heritage. Land hunger and subsistence farming where man had to break his back to produce a survival diet, with either terraces or lazy beds, were common experiences and further united us. A clan society dominated by powerful chiefs and callous landlords was as well known to the Nepalese hillboys as it was to Gaeldom. The love of partying with dance, drink and song does not exist in most of Nepal's surrounding countries but the Nepalese have made it part of their social culture and my colleagues enthusiastically embraced it when encountered in the Western Isles. The boys felt completely at home in the Hebrides; the biggest indicator of the trip's success.

For me the Outer Hebrides had been as magical as I could have hoped; I don't think I've seen as much blue, yellow and white in nature. If there was ever a flag to be designed for the Isles it would have to carry a blonde beach strip of cream, a deep-sea turquoise and a bright sky blue. Perhaps there would be room for a green bar dotted with yellow to represent the machair. It might sound a mess, but it would capture the Isles' predominant colours. I, for one, was just about blued out.

Arrival in Edinburgh saw our story suddenly end where the trip had begun: at Redford Barracks. Not only was it time to say goodbye to Suk, Nugendra, Kesh and Ram but Dhal too. Our dashing sergeant was staying with Ram's family before heading back to England the following day. We shook hands with a mixture of sadness and utter satisfaction. It was not the end of our friendships, of course. Suk met Ewen and me many times in his remaining months in Scotland's capital, while we met Ram's family and Kesh at Dashain a few months later. It took two whole years before a big Gurkha came out of the night when I was visiting Sandhurst. 'Neil?' came a voice. It was Nugendra. Yes, he had learned to drive and use PowerPoint, plus his English had improved, but no, he hadn't married. Dhal, though, has left the Army and now lives in Nuneaton with his family. We meet up from time to time. Dhal has to come to Scotland occasionally simply to maintain his piping equilibrium and always has a welcome spare room in my flat.

'Neil Saheb?' asked Suk. 'If you write about this, you won't forget me, will you?'

'Suk,' I promised. 'I'll open and finish the book with you!'

'I believe you.' Fine words and as profoundly meant as the man himself – and his type.

Also by Neil Griffiths

Gurkha Reiver
Walking the Southern Upland Way

'The funniest book I've read about the modern Gurkha.' **Joanna Lumley**

'Griffiths' fondness for the Gurkhas radiates every page ... Buy this book.' ***Dumfries and Galloway Standard.***

'Engaging ... normally I do not approve of treks, mountaineering and so on, but I am willing to bend my stern code on this occasion.' **Rab McNeil, *The Scotsman***

'His story fairly gallops along, rather like his four colleagues and Griffiths himself.' **Fordyce Maxwell, *The Scotsman***

'Bound to inspire walkers. Seamlessly stitches history with travelogue ... wryly amusing... ***Focus***

ISBN 0-9544416-0-5 £10.99 Royalties go to the Gurkha Welfare Trust

Gurkha Highlander
Walking Mallaig to Stonehaven

' A hilarious, touching account of Gurkhas trekking across Scotland. I laughed out loud. Buy it!' **Joanna Lumley**

'Some people are just plain writers. Neil Griffiths tells it like it is – only better.' ***The Scots Magazine***

''The only oeuvre that brings together Joanna Lumley, Queen Victoria, Kirsty Wark, Kate Adie and Bonnie Prince Charlie ... it has terrific photographs snapped by Griffiths himself.' **Simon Pia, *The Scotsman***

'No ordinary travelogue ... hilarity ensues ... both poignant and laugh-out-loud funny. ***Scotland Magazine***

ISBN 0-9544416-3-X £10.99 Royalties go to the Gurkha Welfare Trust

Cualann Press Limited, 6 Corpach Drive, Dunfermline, Fife KY12 7XG
Tel/Fax 01383 733724
Email: cualann@btinternet.com Website: www.cualann.com